ROBERT A.M. STERN
1965-1980

ROBERT A.M. STERN
1965-1980

Toward a Modern Architecture after Modernism

Edited by Peter Arnell and Ted Bickford

RIZZOLI
NEW YORK

Published in the United States of America in 1981 by

RIZZOLI INTERNATIONAL PUBLICATIONS, INC.
712 Fifth Avenue, New York, 10019

LC: 81-51235
ISBN: 0-8478-0400-3

Reprinted 1984, 1987

The interview that appears on pages 244-249 was
reprinted with permission of Daniel Schneider.
This interview originally appeared on page 34-39 in
Columbia University's *Upstart Journal*, Spring, 1981.

Printed and bound in Singapore
Designed by Arnell/Bickford Associates, New York City

Table of Contents

Selected Works

Foreword

Of the group of younger architects now risen to prominence, Robert Stern is the preeminent exponent of stylistic freedom. He is a master of architectural drama, with a number of well rehearsed roles in his repertoire, each delivered in relationship to a uniquely honed sensitivity to place and occasion. When the Muse whispers, he's a willing accomplice, and sketching a script in a language once thought to have been categorically defunct, Stern is no mere mouthpiece of the past; he makes sure to allow himself some extensive monologues of his own invention. Backstage in his office, he can be seen assembling odd fragments, composing and recomposing the parts into constructs whose meanings go far beyond mere illustration toward archetypal experience.

Where lesser courage would have failed, an indomitable spirit has sustained Stern in this rich scenario for almost two decades. The intrepid young man, whose interest in history wrought creases in the steely composure of the modernist instructors at Yale, has matured into a performer with a big voice. Those early days at Yale were seminal ones for Stern whose remarkable student editorial effort, the 1965 issue of PERSPECTA 9/10 brought together in one journal the theories and buildings of Venturi, Kahn and Moore and presented them as independent manifestations of a common theme. Time has confirmed the accuracy of this prognosis. Stern himself has gone on to become the eminent polemicist and *agent-provocateur* of the Post-Modern movement. Today, he continues the dialogue whose ideological parameters he was so instrumental in defining.

As a writer and teacher, Stern's committment to criticism and history endures. But this hasn't detached him from the realistic exigencies of a demanding practice nor from a sense of professional responsibility. Always the consummate New Yorker, his sense of affiliation with this immediate environment is binding. As president of the Architectural League of New York, he restored that failing body to its previously creditable role as a forum for architectural thought and discussion. Later, through his participation in various programs at the Institute for Architecture and Urban Studies, whose distant view of the American architectural tradition was legend in the 1970s, he helped consolidate a climate of open dialogue.

The Metropolitan context has provided Stern a rich source of patronage. Like Stanford White and Philip Johnson before him, Stern has an implicit understanding of the workings and desires of his urbane, elite clientele. Though to date they have restricted him largely to projects of residential scale, he has never disappointed them or their ambitions.

Then there is the work itself. It's a quintessentially American pragmatism that wants to implement words with a more substantive mode of expression. From the earliest projects to the most recent, critical activity has found an effective analogue in the built product. The variety of idioms reveal a mind that's sometimes playful, but always inquiring. This is a pluralist with a conscience.

Clearly, the forms of the work are not generated *ex vacuo*. Rather, in a strategy consistent with eclectic convictions, they are drawn from the collective formal repertoire. Stern's largesse in acknowledging his sources, whether historical, indigenous, or current, and the spirit of personal cooperation which characterizes his office (he is also known for the generous way in which he acknowledges the assistance of individuals in his office) confirms his confidence in the mechanism by which tradition is transmitted from one generation to the next. His method is a dynamic model for extending and expanding an acquired culture. If the resultant forms don't always resonate with a desired vibrancy, their intentions at least are always extremely clear. Stern, like Philip Johnson, represents an active link with an earlier generation. Through Stern, we are led to a past that cannot but help enrich all our capacities for action in the present.

Peter Arnell
Ted Bickford

Toward a Modern Architecture
After Modernism

Robert A.M. Stern

"The intelligent use, adaptation, and development of traditional forms makes constant demands upon originality and good judgment." Werner Hegemann and Elbert Peets, *Civic Art* (NY, 1922) p. 107

I am pleased that an internationally recognized book seller and publisher and two young architects have combined their energies to afford me an opportunity to take a retrospective look at my work as I enter that period of life generally regarded as an architect's first maturity. While at the age of forty-two I may no longer be considered a "young architect", I fully expect to continue to be what I have always been—a student of architecture in all its aspects. At this moment, as the materialist and pseudo-scientific values of the modern architecture of the previous 30 years or so are everywhere being questioned, I feel myself very much in touch with a larger movement than any one architect's work can encompass, a broad-based ground-swell of belief that promises to restore to architecture its traditions, and thereby its rightful place in the world of ideas. Le Corbusier observed in the introduction to the first edition of his *Oeuvre Complete:* "I do not believe that all architecture which speaks to the soul is always the work of individuals. A man here, another there, perceives, understands, makes a decision and proceeds to act, to create. And as a result a solution emerges which enables other men to grasp their own bent or find their true direction."

As I believe profoundly in the continuity of tradition, I search for the signs of its persistence in the present: I search the contemporary scene for icons of permanence and I do my best to use them in order to foster a sense of my work as an anchor in the effluvia of current production. I try to make the outward manifestations of change comprehensible by entering into a dialogue with the past, with tradition. Is this search not the essence of architecture, of all culture in fact?

The differences in architectural expression from person to person, from time to time, are not only the trivialities of passing fashion but also the reflection of each era's conception of its own place in tradition. While I admire the abstract aspect of architecture—that is its underlying compositional principles—I cannot help being impressed by the capacity for architecture to break its own rules.

While I treasure my time as a practicing architect, I also need time to explore other interests within its discipline. To be a professional—that is to do something one loves as opposed merely to do a job—seems the greatest privilege imaginable. For me, to profess architecture is to profess its present as well as its past, to know about its origins in a scholarly way and to make new buildings. The intimacy of scholarly contact with the past refreshes me as I contemplate the problems of the moment.

Much of my effort and that of my colleagues during the past fifteen years has been expended on quite small things; on the whole ours has been more a practice of "modest interventions" rather than one of "bold propositions". Yet each occasion for design is always accompanied by a renewed sense of the power of ideas, no matter how modestly expressed, to move one's fellows, particularly if these ideas can gain strength by virtue of new associations with experiences deeply rooted in the culture.

Architecture cannot flourish so long as architects believe they stand before a *tabula rasa,* so long as they believe that the individual building is principally the product of individual talent and individual personality. Architecture is a synthesis of traditional values and immediate circumstance. The particular synthesis each architect makes is in effect the definition of who he or she is and what he or she believes: that is our personal moral responsibility.

This book provides an occasion to take a broad view, to record but not, let us hope, sum up, the ideas that inform my work, work that I immodestly believe can serve to some extent as a symbol for the very many of us who embrace an architecture that self-consciously addresses issues of culture through the vehicle of aesthetics. Too often, the search for an architecture that is committed to the communication of "meaning" in the way that we expect literature and the other arts to be, is presented in the press as something apart from a concern for "aesthetics." Such is a false split and, as I hope the work will demonstrate, the struggle to transform the every day into the poetic—to make beautiful shapes and places, to amaze and even to inspire is still the essential architectural act. While the work has never lived up to my own expectations for it, I cannot but express that the struggle to inspire such feelings has always guided the process.

What I am saying can be put in another way; for me the pleasure in architecture is not fulfilled merely in the design of buildings and their settings for their own sake—what Le Corbusier ineffably characterized as the "play of forms under the light" —but requires that those forms incorporate the memory of buildings and settings from one's own past and from the past in general, from culture. This can be seen as a kind of nostalgia, not the easy kind of manufactured memory that one finds in the commercial marketplace but a more serious commitment to one's individual experience as an artist and to the qualities and characteristics of the cultural milieu for which the work is to be made. Our task is to open ourselves up to our own personal past and to the cultural past as well; to know who we are we must know who we were and where we are.

Perhaps to know where we are is all we can ever know. I became an architect because I loved the buildings of my city, New York and imagined one day that I would make ones like them—not the same ones, but ones that like them were imbued with the spirit of confidence and the dignity of the best of them. I have never been very far from my city, and it has held me in a child-like thrall for twenty-five or more years. The New York of my youth is to this day the principal subject of all my work in architecture.

The contents of this volume, documenting independent work in design over fifteen years, fall into two chronologically related groupings which can be described, however blushingly, as belonging to times of "youth" and "early maturity". The first period extending from the completion of my formal training at Yale in 1965, is not only preoccupied with the establishment of professional credentials but with the beginning search for a richness of expression in design that would be commensurate with my already far more developed critical sense of the issues. That search, going in a number of directions, was however limited by my inability to perceive that the only effective way to enrich my architectural vocabulary without resorting to undue oddities of shape-making was to break free of the inherently limiting conception of architecture which I then had, one which has been presented to me as the only one or at least the best or most appropriate one available to us in the twentieth century, one which was described sweepingly—presumptively even, and I believe erroneously—as *modern architecture*. Thus the work of my first ten years of practice should be seen as an attempt to expand from within by returning to the example of the early masters of modernism, especially the forms of invention of Le Corbusier and the spatial complexities of Frank Lloyd Wright (both of which are marvelously synthesized in the work of my teacher Paul Rudolph). It is to Rudolph more than to any other that I owe my sense of myself as an architect; it was he who opened up my eyes to seeing (as opposed to mere looking) and not only made it clear that every work of architecture has a lesson in it, but that every architect is obliged to take on each and every project offered and to do his level best to achieve architecture with it. Most importantly of all, Rudolph, seated at my desk for a "crit" was able to pore over my inchoate jottings and not only see things I had made but could not see but also be able to direct me toward the realization of ideas I did not know I had.

By paying very close attention to the written and built work of Robert Venturi in the late 1960s and early '70s, the door was opened for me to what I believe is a larger view of architecture, one which is now leading to the second phase of my development, one in which I imagine myself to be as yet quite fully immersed, one marked by a growing awareness that the way to enrich the communicative capacity of architecture is to break with the model of what had been regarded as modern architecture—that is the model of modernism—and to attempt a synthesis between current problems and techniques and traditional values. In attempting to break with the modernist model—or at the very least to understand how its ideals came to be formulated—I have become increasingly aware of the on-going tradition of Modern architecture and of its broad, deep connections to our everyday experience.

I believe that three paradigms—or perhaps more correctly, the interaction between three paradigms—characterize Modern architecture: the classical paradigm, the vernacular paradigm and the process or production paradigm. The classical paradigm is concerned with the grammar, syntax and rhetoric of what is generally called the classical language—arguably the language and tradition of Western architectural culture. The classical paradigm takes the compositional methods and the basic forms of the Graeco-Roman world as the model for an architecture that attempts to be at once rational (mathematical) and humanistic (natural). The vernacular paradigm is based on a belief that the classical paradigm is elitist and that the architecture of the Modern world should find a local basis for form. This paradigm uses the example of everyday life to combat the expressionless cliches into which an overdependence on the other two paradigms can lead. The vernacular paradigm enriches architecture with forms that are culturally specific. The process paradigm represents an attempt to establish a model for those conditions which are distinctly those of the Modern era, the world of mass populations and industrialized production. The process paradigm keeps a basis for form in the constituent facts of building productions and in an idealized conception of the possibilities of serial production in Western culture. Since architecture, as opposed to mere building, is a representation of and not a direct expression of reality it is, therefore, an art. Thus the relationship between actual architectural production and each of these traditions or modes—the classical, the vernacular and the technological—is symbolic, and it is this symbolic relationship that gives the three modes their paradigmatic nature in the design process.

The work beginning in the Lang House is a measure of my growing recognition of the Modern condition in architecture. Each project since that house can be seen as the product of a self-conscious effort to discover within the conditions of program, site and available technique clues that would trigger a meaningful discourse between the present and the past, between the requirements of the moment and the paradigms of Modern experience.

Design is, in part, a process of cultural assimilation. Though it includes problem-solving, the functional and technological strategies for the vast majority of situations with which we deal are established. Our task is to question the seemingly unique problems which dog us at any given moment by examining them in relationship to the paradigms which have characterized our architectural tradition for at least 500 years. And such questioning can come not only from the wellspring of our individual 'talent', but also from a knowledge of that history, a concern for the state of the architectural art at a given moment, a serious respect for the aspirations and intelligence of clients and the society that permits us to function at all. It must be continuously reaffirmed that individual buildings, no matter how remotely situated from other works of architecture, form part of a cultural and physical context. What is more, we are obliged to acknowledge these connections not only in our words, but also in deeds. Architecture must live up to its representational role if it is to survive; architecture is not package design.

As a culture, as architects, we know so very much. What must be done is to face this knowledge squarely—and in so doing, face the world around us, taking it for what it is, incrementally adapting the objects and ideas in it to our needs while we in turn adapt to its demands. My attitude toward form, based on a love for and a knowledge of history, is not concerned with accurate replication. It is eclectic and uses collage and juxtaposition as techniques to give new meaning to familar shapes and, in so doing to cover new ground. Mine is a confidence in the power of memory (history) combined with the action of people (function) to infuse design with richness and meaning. If architecture is to succeed in its efforts to participate creatively in the present, it must go beyond the inconoclasm of the modern movement and recapture for itself a basis in culture and the fullest possible reading of its own past.

I have written these words and formulated these projects in a belief that modernism as a movement in literature and the visual arts has run its course. But, at the same time, I wish to suggest that Modern architecture, viewed in the broad way remains a viable proposition. As a Modern (architect) I cannot but remain a child of the Enlightenment; I recognize the demands placed in culture by new programs, and new techniques; yet I cannot allow myself to be trapped in the present.

A word or two about how I work. In 1969 I entered into partnership with John Hagmann, whom I had first known in New Haven when we were both students. Since New Haven Hagmann had worked in London and in the offices of I.M. Pei and Edward Larrabee Barnes while I had during that time worked briefly for Richard Meier, a little on my own, designing the Wiseman house, and for over two years in the Housing and Development Administration of the City of New York.

In our seven year partnership, Hagmann and I forged together the basic organization and attitude which characterizes the independent practice which I have since continued (Hagmann is now associated with a large firm specializing in commercial projects). Increasingly, our office pursues individual projects that are likely to be realized, but also attempts to explore other issues of a more theoretical nature. In particular, we have worked out plans for suburbs and for the buildings which would permit them to be inhabited in order to demonstrate our belief that the one genuine urbanistic invention of the Modern era has been shockingly neglected in the last 50 years by architects and urban planners, and that its time has come to once again take its place in our architecture.

In all these efforts I have been fortunate to have the collaboration of others, especially a marvelously understanding structural engineer, Robert Silman. I also count among my valued collaborators Carroll Cline, lighting designer and Peter G. Rolland, landscape architect. Most of all, without the enthusiastic dedication of the excellent assistants in the office over the years, very many of them former students of mine at Columbia and Yale, none of the work in this book could have been realized.

Chronological List of Projects

1965-1967
Wiseman House, Montauk, New York

1967-1968
Stern Apartment I, New York, New York

1967-1968
Stern Apartment II, New York, New York

1968-1969
Residence, East Hampton, New York

1968
Gimbel Apartment, New York, New York

1969
Showroom and Offices for Tiffeau-Busch,
New York, New York

1969
Seiniger House, Westhampton, New York

1969-1970
Showrooms for Helen Harper, Inc.,
New York, New York

1969-1970
Office Addition, Long Island, New York

1969-1971
White/Hoffman Apartment, New York,
New York

1970
Jenkins House, East Hampton, New York

1970
Kozmopolitan Gallery, New York, New York

1970-1971
Traveling Exhibition, *Another Chance for
Cities*

1970-1971
Poolhouse, Purchase, New York

1971
Roberts Apartment, New York, New York

1971
Geary Brownstone, New York, New York

1971-1972
Kretchmer Apartment, New York, New York

1971-1972
Residence, Montauk, New York

1971
Residence, Gladwynne, Pennsylvania

1972-1979
New York Brownstone, New York, New York

1973
Howard Apartment, New York, New York

1973
Rooftop Apartment, New York, New York

1973
House Beautiful Living Center

1973
Duplex Apartment, New York, New York

1973-1975
Residence, East Hampton, New York

1973
Residence, Greenwich, Connecticut

1973
Marks/Friedman Apartment, New York,
New York

1973
Offices for Source Securities Corporation,
New York, New York

1973
The Architects Offices, New York, New York

1973
Godsick Apartment, New York, New York

1973-1974
Lang Residence, Connecticut

1973-1974
Poolhouse, Greenwich, Connecticut

1974
Middleton Apartment, New York, New York

1974
Model Apartment, Olympic Tower,
New York, New York

1974
House Addition, Purchase, New York

1974
Library, Museum and Civic Plaza, Biloxi,
Mississippi

1974-1976
Residence, Westchester County, New York

1974-1975
New York Townhouse, New York City

1975
Regina Rail Center, Saskatchewan, Canada

1975
Collector's Apartment, New York

1975
Residence, North Stamford, Connecticut

1975
Roosevelt Island Competition, New York City

1975
Jerome Greene Hall, Columbia University

1975-1976
Residence, Eastern Long Island, New York

1975
Apartment, Elkins Park, Pennsylvania

1976-1977
Residence, Mount Desert Island, Maine

1976
Riviera Beach Suburb, Singer Island, Florida
1976
Killington Ski Lodge, Killington, Vermont
1976
Minnesota State House Extension, Minneapolis
1976
Singer House Renovation, Stamford, Connecticut
1976
Student Lounge, Uris Hall, Columbia University
1976
Association House Apartments, New York, New York
1976
Peaceable Kingdom Barn, Texas
1976-1980
Subway Suburb; Venice Biennale, Italy
1976
Housing for the Elderly, Brookhaven, New York
1977
Park Avenue Apartment, New York, New York
1977
10th Anniversary Poster, I.A.U.S.
1977-1978
Residence, Fairfield County, Connecticut
1977
Fifth Avenue Apartment, New York, New York
1977
Reinhold Child's Room, New York, New York
1977-1978
Residence, Deal, New Jersey
1978
Erbun Fabrics Showroom, New York City
1978
First Avenue Squash Club, New York City
1978
Redtop, Dublin, New Hampshire
1978-1980
Furniture Design, Griffin Table
1978
Fresh Cafe, New York, New York
1979
Cottage, East Hampton

1979
Summer Residence, East Hampton, New York
1979
Gramercy Park Apartment, New York City
1979
International House, New York City
1979
Super Spa Bathing Pavilion
1979-1980
Inner Dune Residence, East Hampton
1979-1980
Residence, Llewellyn Park, New Jersey
1979
Residence, East Hampton, New York
1979
Best Products Catalog Showroom
1979-1981
Lawson Residence, East Quogue, New York
1979
Temple of Love, East Hampton
1979-1980
Medical Offices, New York, New York
1979-1980
Contractor's Offices, Long Island City, New York
1979-1980
Residence, King's Point, New York
1979
Visitor's Center, Shaker Village, Kentucky
1980
Medical Loft, New York, New York
1980
Broadway Loft, New York, New York
1980
Furniture Designs, Tuscan Table
1980
Prototype Housing, Long Island, New York
1980
Residence, Childmark, Massachusetts
1980
Saper House Addition, Woodstock, New York
1980
Venice Biennale Facade, Venice, Italy
1980
Chicago Tribune Competition, Late Entry
1980
Classical Duplex Apartment, New York, New York

1980
Ferris Booth Hall, Columbia University
1980
City Hall Annex, Cincinnati, Ohio
1980
Southern California Institute of Art Exhibition
1980
East End Avenue Apartment, New York, New York
1980
Tower House, East Hampton, New York
1980-1981
Residence, Farm Neck, Massachusetts
1980
Garibaldi Meucci Museum Competition
1980
Scaling Modernism, Collaboration with Robert Graham
1980
D.O.M. Corporation Headquarters, Bruhl, Germany
1980
Residence, East Hampton, Long Island
1980-1981
Residence, Locust Valley, New York
1980
Library, San Juan Capistrano, California
1980
Offices, Catlin and Cox, New York, New York
1980
Design Pavilion, Linz, Austria
1980-1981
Madison Avenue Apartment, New York City
1981
Residence, Shelter Island, New York
1980-1981
Young-Hoffman Exhibition, Chicago, Illinois
1981
Richmond Centre, Richmond, Virginia
1980-1981
Two Houses for Corbel Properties East Hampton, New York
1981
Mecox Field, Bridgehampton, New York
1981
House Renovation, King's Point, New York

Biographical Data

1939	Born May 23, in New York City
1960	Columbia University, B.A.
1965	Yale University, M. Architecture
1965-1966	Program Director, The Architectural League of New York
1966	Designer, Office of Richard Meier, Architect
1966-1967	Consultant to Philip Johnson for "Eye on New York", television documentary on New York City planning, CBS-TV.
1967-1970	Member, John V. Lindsay's Task Force on Urban Design
1966-1970	Consultant, Small Parks Program, Department of Parks, City of New York City of New York
1967-1970	Urban Designer and Assistant (for Design Policy) to Assistant Administrator Samuel Ratensky, Housing and Development Administration, the City of New York.
1967-1979	Trustee, American Federation of the Arts
1969-1973	Vice President, Cunningham Dance Foundation
1969-1977	Partner, Robert A.M. Stern and John S. Hagmann Architects
1970-1976	Architecture Committee, Whitney Museum of American Art
1973-1977	President, Architectural League of New York
1974-1977	Adviser, Program for Continuing Education in Architecture, Institute for Architecture and Urban Studies
1975-1978	Member, Board of Directors, Society of Architectural Historians
1977-	Editorial Consultant, Architectural History Foundation
1977-	Principal, Robert A.M. Stern Architects (Successors to Stern & Hagmann)

Significant Lectures and Symposia:

"**The Shape of Cities in Our Time**", five evening symposium held at the Museum of Modern Art, Spring 1966;

"**White/Grey/Silver**", Conference on Architecture, University of California at Los Angeles, May 1974;

"**State of the Art of Architecture in 1977**", Graham Foundation for Advanced Studies in the Fine Arts, Chicago, Illinois, October 25, 1977;

"**Design in Transition**", American Institute of Architects Convention, Dallas, Texas, May 24, 1978;

"**Summer Institute on Energy Conscious Design**", American Institute of Architects Research Corporation, Harvard Graduate School of Design, July 28-August 4, 1978;

"**Louis I. Kahn as a Teacher**", The Drawing Center, New York, September 6, 1978;

1978 Central States Regional Conference, Iowa State University, Ames, Iowa, October 8-10, 1978;

"**Beauty in Architecture**", Keynote address, Association of Collegiate Schools of Architecture, Regional Conference, University of Kansas, Lawrence, Kansas, October 19, 1978;

"**Alternatives**", The NERC/AIA Conference, a Seminar/Debate concerning the Art of Architecture, Dartmouth College, Hanover, New Hampshire, October 21, 1978;

"**Directions**", Washington University, St. Louis, Missouri, November 6, 1978;

Chairman 1978-1979 Association of Collegiate School of Architecture-American Institute of Architects (ACSA-AIA) Teachers Seminar Committee at Cranbrook, Michigan, June 1979;

"**City Segments**", Walker Art Center, Minneapolis, April 19-20, 1980

Teaching Positions

Columbia University:
Lecturer, 1969-72;
Assistant Professor, 1972-77;
Associate Professor, 1977-;
College Departmental Representative, 1973-;
Chairman, Committee on Lectures and Exhibits, 1971-81;

Yale University:
Visiting Lecturer, 1972, 1973;
William Henry Bishop Visiting Professor, 1978;

University of Houston:
Visiting Critic, September 1974;

Mississippi State University:
Design Critic, November 1974;

Rhode Island School of Design:
Visiting Critic, November-December 1976;

University of Pennsylvania, Graduate School of Fine Arts, Department of Architecture:
Visiting Critic, Fall 1977;

North Carolina State University, Raleigh, N.C.:
Visiting Distinguished Critic, Spring 1978;

University of North Carolina, Charlotte, N.C.:
Visiting Critic, 1979;

Rice University, Houston:
Visiting Critic, Spring 1979;

ASC/AIA, Cranbrook Academy Seminar, Bloomfield Hills, Michigan.
Organizer, 1979;

Institute for Architecture and Urban Studies, New York, N.Y.
Visiting Critic, 1980.

17

1965-1967

Wiseman House · Montauk · New York

A year-round vacation house for a growing family, this house sits on a high wooded site overlooking the ocean and the beach as it stretches toward Amagansett. Within the overall discipline of the gable shape, a variety of spaces surrounds a two and one half storey high entrance hall. Living areas are raised for the view. A roof deck above the tree tops provides a sweeping vista of ocean and bay. The contrast between the front and rear elevations is a direct response to the orientation, the view, and the character of the site, which is visible from a great distance and calls for a big scale on the south.

1. General view looking south
2. West elevation
3. General view looking northeast

1

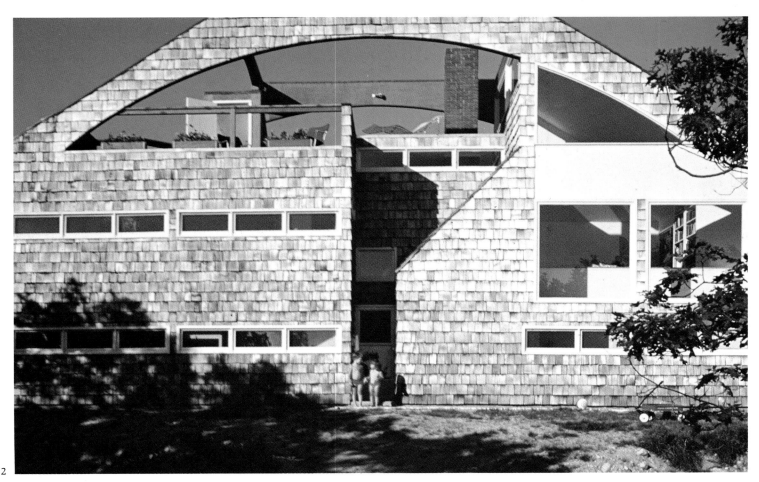

2

3

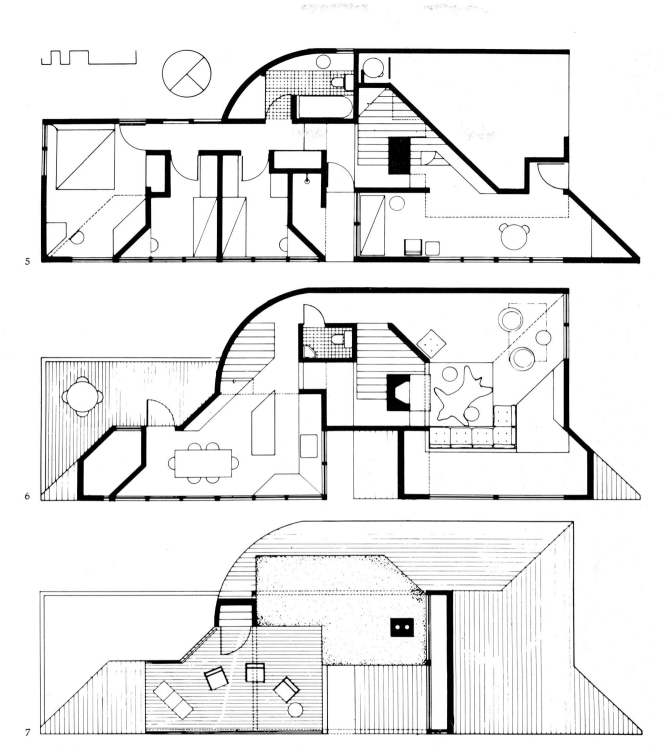

5

6

7

4. Fireplace
5. First floor plan
6. Second floor plan
7. Roof terrace plan

8. Roof detail
9. Living room looking south

6

7

1973

Duplex Apartment · New York City

This long and narrow 50 year old duplex apartment has been completely renovated in accord with the lifestyle of a young family that has particular interests in art. A chopped up plan of many small rooms strung along rather long and gloomy corridors has been considerably simplified, providing for three master bedrooms and reading and entertaining spaces for both adults and children. Two new staircases connect the floors: one leads from the kitchen to the children's bedrooms, and the other connects the major living spaces on the lower floor with the master bedroom and sitting room. This main staircase provides the major statement of verticality in the scheme and its impact is extended through the use of cabinetwork connecting the library, living and dining rooms. Two gentle curves relieve the severity of the rectilinear organization and shorten the apparent length of the apartment.

1. Staircase looking south
2. Axonometric
3. Hallway looking east
4. Upper floor plan
5. Lower floor plan

1

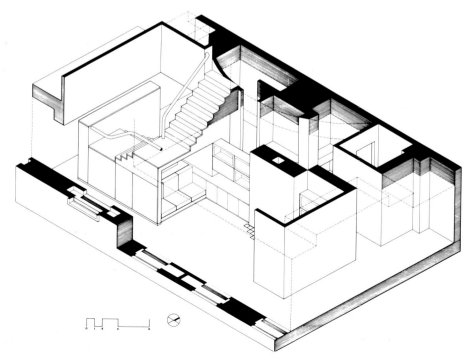

2

3

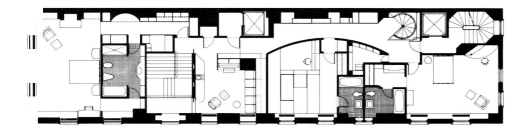

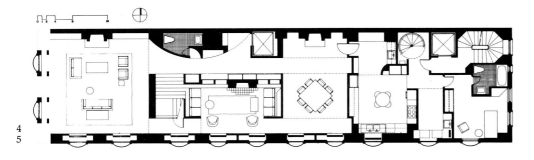

4
5

6

7

6. General view of living room
7. Staircase looking north
8. Family room
9. Staircase looking west

8

9

1973-1975

Residence · East Hampton · New York

The house incorporates parts of the foundations, platform, and partitioning system of a 1950's ranch house. Major contextual factors in forming the design include the problems of noise and privacy, generated by the property's frontage along a main road, and by the shift in axes between the property's planting and the most desirable orientation towards the view and sun.

For these reasons, the house is conceived of as a wall against the street, with principal living spaces and the master bedroom situated on the second floor. The introduction of the diagonal in the plan is a response to the questions of orientation.

The outside is sheathed in two kinds of shingles: on the roof hand-split shingles are used, on the walls the shingles are machine-cut to provide a more delicate and lighter colored surface. Inside, bleached wooden columns and moldings are introduced to enrich the palette. There is no air conditioning; large panes of fixed glass are confined to emphasize major views, while French doors are used for ventilation. Where the French doors occur on the second floor, brass railings are projected to make each opening a miniature balcony.

1. General view looking northwest
2. View looking southwest at entrance
3. Living room looking west
4. Site Plan

1

2

3

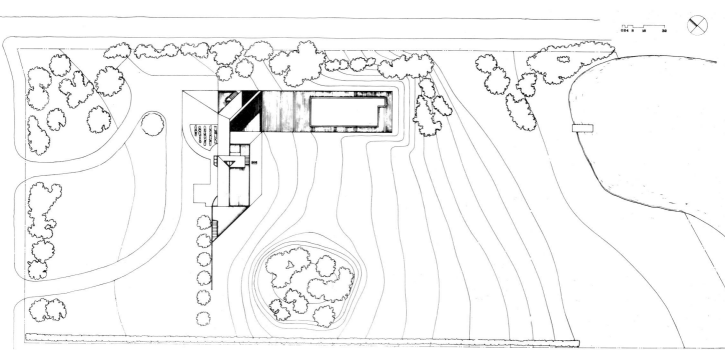

4

5

6

7

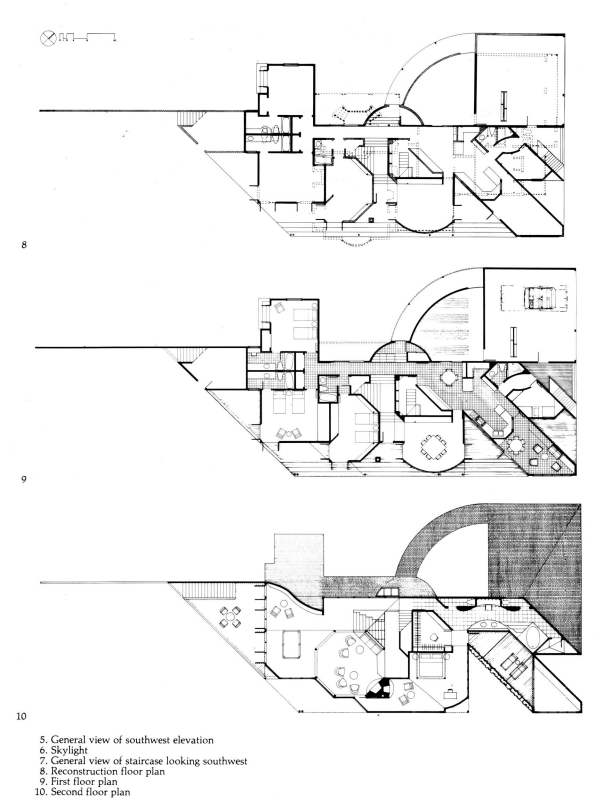

8

9

10

5. General view of southwest elevation
6. Skylight
7. General view of staircase looking southwest
8. Reconstruction floor plan
9. First floor plan
10. Second floor plan

1972-1979

Brownstone · New York City

This renovation involved the relocation of accessways to the upper apartments to allow a more open plan for the owner's triplex apartment at the bottom. The design solution involves a complex layering of major and minor spaces along the longitudinal axis, using exaggerated structure to define rooms and circulation routes. The structural frame continues out into the rear court in response to engineering requirements and to heighten the impact of the spatial ordering of the design without getting in the way of routine use.

The brownstone's new facade expresses at ground level the dual nature of the building's space allocation: the owner's apartment with three floors of rental apartments above. The paneled grey stucco finish recalls the coursing and color of the masonry of the grander Edwardian townhouse adjacent to our project on the east, while the obvious thinness of the finish is more in keeping with the typical brownstone facades on the west.

1. Roof terrace
2. Section through Apartment looking west
3. Dining room looking north from terrace
4. Street elevation
5. Dressing room

1

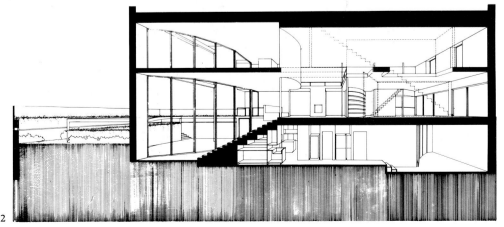

6. View from roof terrace looking south
7. Roof terrace from dining room
8. Master bedroom
9. Study
10. Living room looking south
11. Street elevation
12. Second floor plan
13. First floor plan
14. Cellar floor plan

2

3

5

4

7

8

9

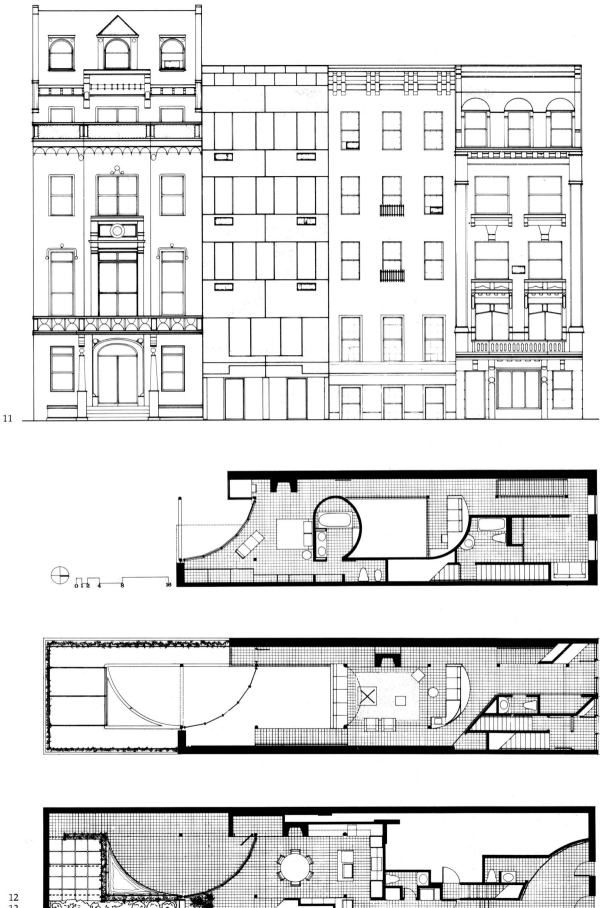

11

12
13
14

7

8

5. View of dining room looking east
6. View of dining room looking west
7. Dining room
8. Foyer

1974-1976

A curving screen wall introduced at the entrance provides for a covered entry, allows for the development of a private outdoor space for the servants, and facilitates the resolution of the diagonal driveway axis with the orthogonal planning of the house itself. On the rear, or garden facade, a bowed screen wall in combination with landscaping serves to reduce the apparent length of the garden elevation, provide integral sun protection, and focus views from the principal interior spaces.

Partly to diminish the apparent size of the house, which has an unusually extensive program, siting and landscaping restrict movement around the ends of the building and force one to move through it to experience it. Episodic organization is the key: the house is conceived as a collection of formal interventions which are assembled by the observer as he moves through the spaces. And the spaces the bounding walls of the house make in the landscape are as important as those which they define in the interior.

The stucco finish of the house, which is both abstract and palpable at the same time, further manifests this quality of connection between the manmade and the natural. A rich cream color capped with terra-cotta colored bands gives a warm quality to the exterior at once reminiscent of Tuscan villas, of Frank Lloyd Wright's Fallingwater and Taliesin North, and of Hollywood in the 1930's.

1. Changing room entrance looking up
2. South elevation screen detail
3. General view of main house
4. Main house looking northwest
5. Gardener's house looking west
6. Main house looking northeast
7. General view of gardener's house looking south

1

8. Pool
9. Site plan
10. View of South elevation
11. Main house living room looking north
12. Master bedroom window wall

2

3

4

6

5

7

Site Plan

0 5 10 20   40

13

14

15

16

17

18

20

21

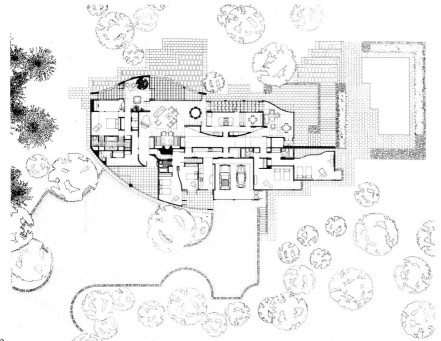

19

13. Changing room
14. Guest bedroom
15. Main house living room looking west
16. Dining room
17. Master bedroom
18. West elevation
19. Main house floor plan
20. Exterior screen
21. Exterior screen
22. Main house north elevation
23. Main house south elevation
24. Axonometric of main house
25. Gardener's cottage north elevation
26. Gardener's cottage south elevation
27. Gardener's cottage floor plan
28. Skylight
29. Skylight

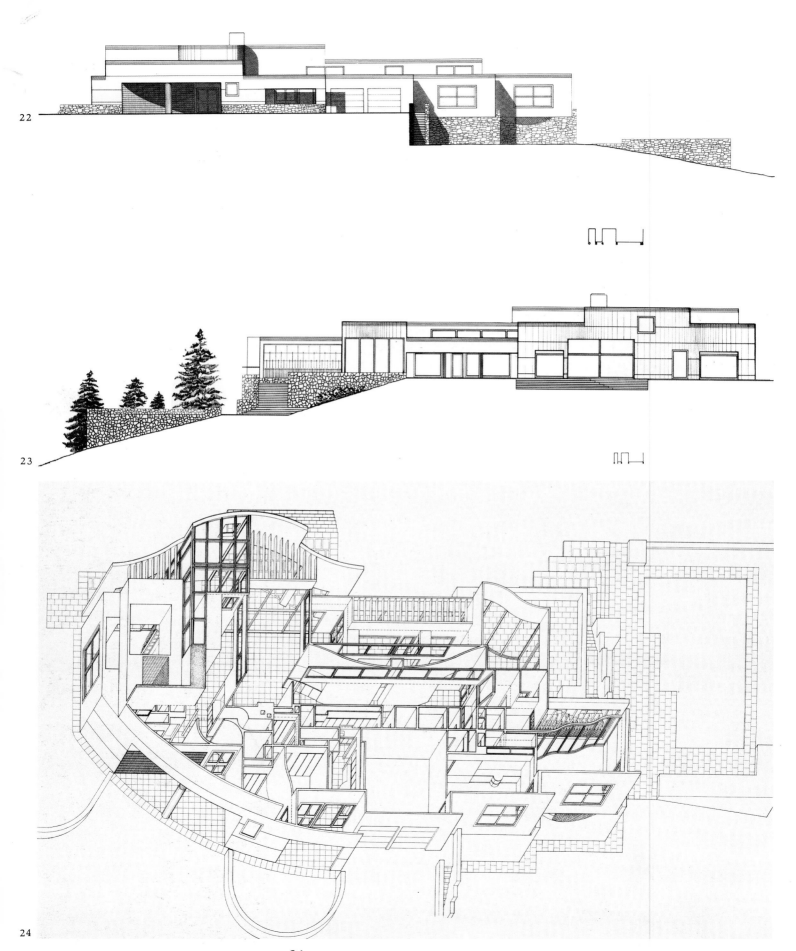

22

23

24

84

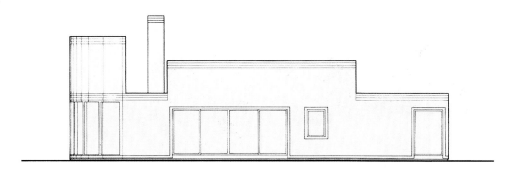

25

Scale 0 1 2 4 8 16

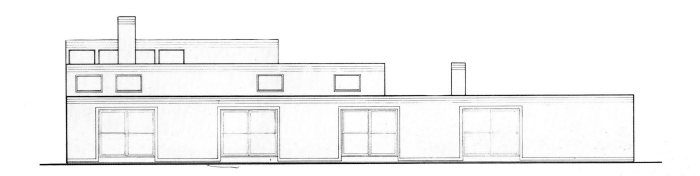

26

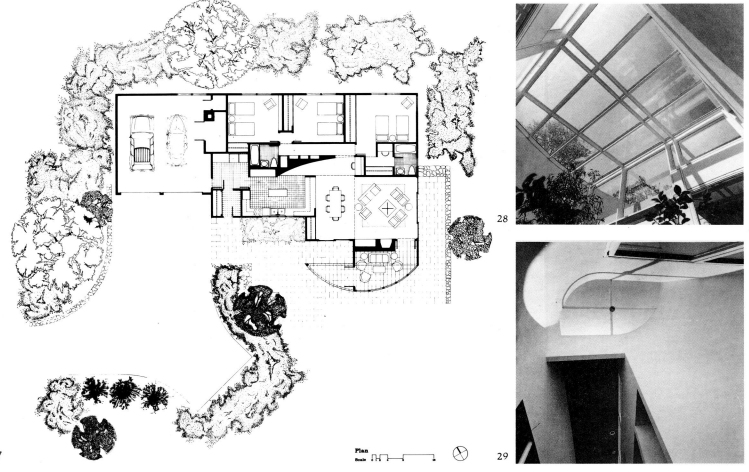

28

27

Plan
Scale

29

1974-1975

New York Townhouse · New York City

A complete reconstruction of a townhouse structure squeezed between large apartment house blocks facing one of New York City's most fashionable avenues, this design deals with issues of privacy, light and orientation within a constrained urban context.

In response to the problems of scale an abstract gridding is introduced alluding to the base/shaft/capital schema of taller neighboring buildings. There are intimations of pilasters at the edges, and a gradual progression in the vertical plane from solid to void, capped by a cornice which appears to be suspended from above. These strategies connect our facade with its neighbors and evoke images of traditional, classicizing townhouse design.

Inside, the major living and entertaining spaces are linked by a "promenade architecturale" extending from the front entrance hall up to the master bedroom suite at the top. A circular stairway toward the rear of the building offers a more direct vertical link, while an elevator provides a third means of circulation. Because of the exceptional depth of the house a four story high atrium is introduced to bring light from monitor windows above and to give an internal focus to the plan and section.

1. Street elevation
2. Street elevation
3. General view looking east

1

2

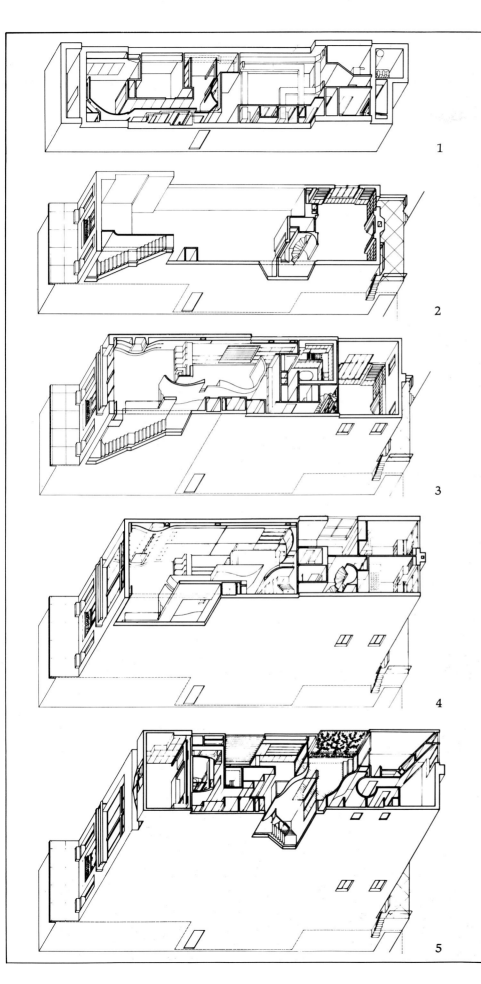

1

2

3

4

5

7

8

9

4. General view looking west
5. Living room looking west
6. Television room looking east
7. Axonometric
8. Exterior roof terrace looking west
9. Living room looking southeast

10. Hallway looking northeast
11. Dining room looking east
12. Dining room looking west
13. Interior view looking east
14. Staircase looking up

15

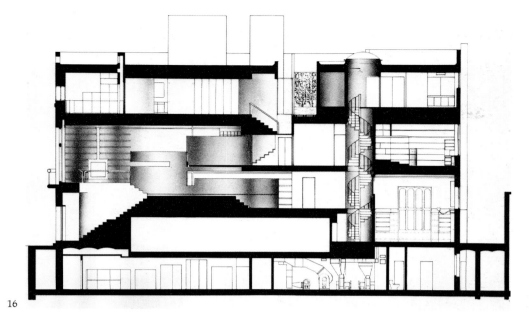

16

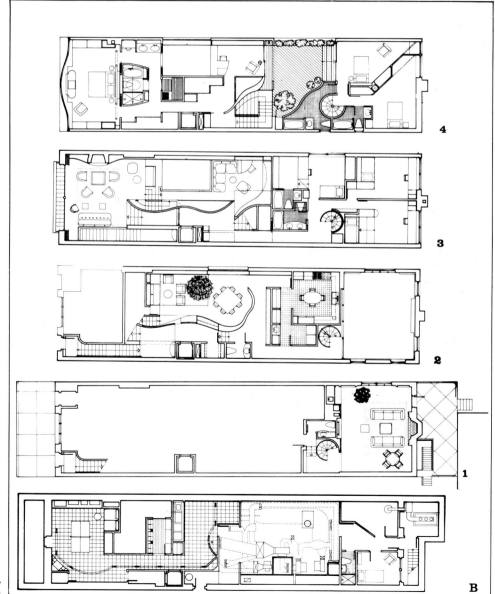

4

3

2

1

B

17
18
19
20
21

15. Living room looking west
16. East-West section
17. Fourth floor plan
18. Third floor plan
19. Second floor plan
20. First floor plan
21. Basement plan

Located in a new, speculatively built suburban apartment building, this apartment accommodates an eclectic collection of furniture and art in a long, narrow area lit only at one edge. The limited palette of finishing materials—white walls, slate floors, neutral fabrics—provides a sympathetic background for the furnishings and objects d'art. Glass block is used to bring natural light to the kitchen located on the interior wall; the swelling shape of its demising wall making particular the various spaces within the long and narrow living room.

1. Master bedroom
2. Entrance foyer looking west
3. Hall looking west
4. Kitchen

5

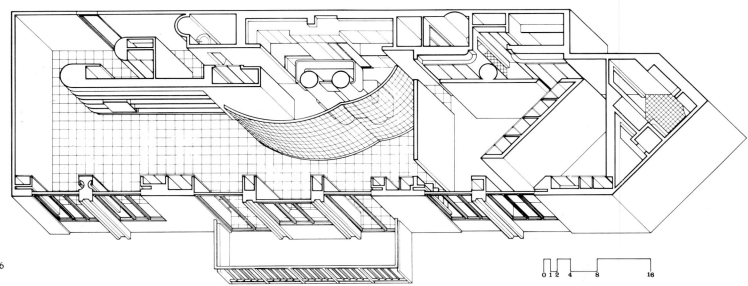

6

0 1 2 4   8   16

7

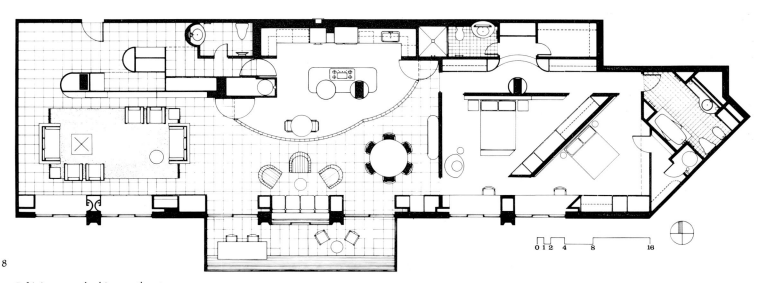

8

5. Living room looking northeast
6. Axonometric
7. Hall and Master bedroom looking east
8. Floor plan

1975

Roosevelt Island Competition · N.Y.

In November 1974, the New York State Urban Development Corporation announced an open competition for housing 1,000 upper, middle, and low income families on an 8.8 acre parcel of land on Roosevelt Island in New York City. Of 250 submissions, ours was awarded first prize.

Our solution introduces a pedestrian street running longitudinally through the site and continuing the diagonal offsets of the street pattern established in earlier stages of the island's development. Our street, "Octagon Way," gives access to the apartments as well as to such various community functions as meeting rooms, a day care center, two public schools, laundry rooms, and an amphitheater. It provides the principal pedestrian gateway to Octagon Park, a major park and recreational area planned for the island.

The three apartment towers are placed at the water's edge to take advantage of river views and to minimize their apparent bulk and the effect of their shadows on the usable open spaces. Almost all apartments have two exposures, and throughout the project there is a wide variety of apartment type. More than one-half of the apartments are accommodated in 6-and 8-story buildings which provide residents with a comfortable relationship to the ground plane, and many have unprogrammed living spaces and private gardens, terraces or balconies. All apartment buildings enter directly from Octagon Way and all townhouse apartments have direct access to it, enhancing the sense of identity and privacy for the individual apartment dweller.

1. Model view looking south
2. Model view looking northeast
3. Model view looking northwest
4. Axonometric
5. Northtown site plan
6. General site plan

1

2

3

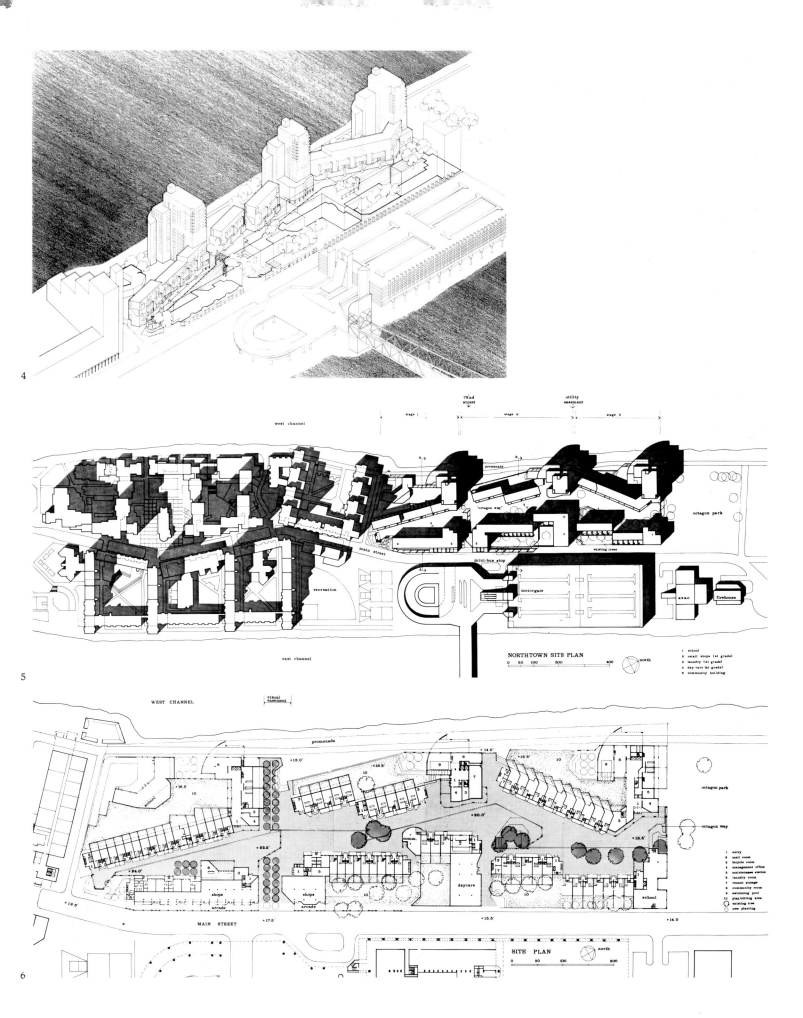

4

west channel

72'nd street

utility easement

stage 1

stage 2

stage 3

promenade

'octagon way'

octagon park

main street

recreation

mini-bus stop

existing trees

motorgate

avac

firehouse

east channel

NORTHTOWN SITE PLAN

0 50 100   200   400

north

1 school
2 retail shops (at grade)
3 laundry (at grade)
4 day care (at grade)
5 community building

5

WEST CHANNEL

visual easement

promenade

+13.0'

+14.0'

+16.5'

8

8

10

10

9

10

school

+16.5'

+16.5'

7

octagon park

10

+20.0'

+18.5'

octagon way

+22.5'

comm.

+24.0'

6

shops

shops

arcade

arcade

daycare

school

+19.5'

MAIN STREET

+17.5'

+15.5'

+14.0

1 entry
2 mail room
3 bicycle room
4 management office
5 maintenance station
6 tenant storage
7 laundry room
8 community room
9 swimming pool
10 play/sitting area
○ existing tree
○ new planting

SITE PLAN

north

0 50   100   200

6

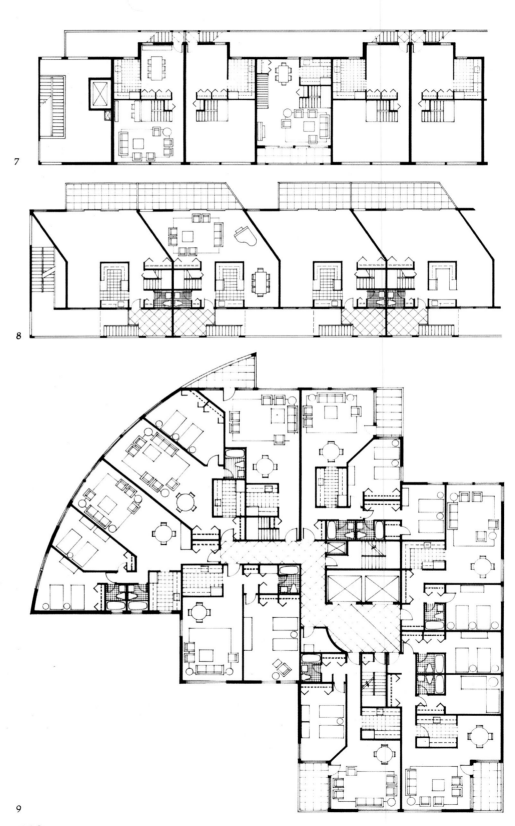

7

8

9

10

7. Lowrise typical floor plan
8. Lowrise typical floor plan
9. Tower typical floor plan
10. Pedestrian walkway
11. Park and highrise buildings

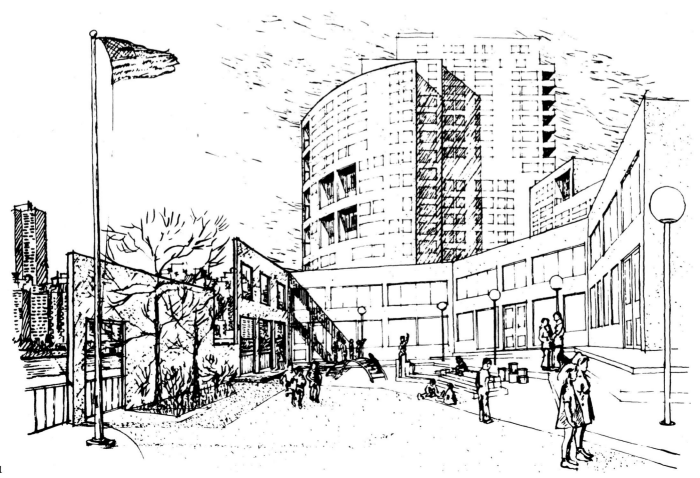

11

13

14

12. General model view looking south
13. Modelview looking west of highrise buildings
14. Modelview looking south

1975

Jerome Greene Hall · Columbia Univ.

The programme at Jerome Greene Hall called for the conversion of the technologically antiquated and aesthetically vandalised facilities of the former Women's Faculty Club and the adjoining surplus residential facilities in Johnson Hall into a student center for the School of Law. Along with a variety of lounge spaces, Greene Hall includes offices, seminar and conference rooms as well as a new bridge to connect with the adjacent Faculty House.

Our design is intended to counterbalance the impersonal abstraction of the principal Law School facility, a building of the late 1950s. It is intended not only to recapture as much as possible of the original character of the club rooms—which were designed in a style best described as etiolated Adam via last-gasp posthumous McKim, Mead and White—but also to extend, revitalise and thereby revive the original vocabulary. The new work at Greene Hall tries to speak the language of the old; ours has been a process of restoration, renovation, and recycling —but not one of remodelling in the literal sense. In short, we see ourselves as architectural re-weavers using deliberately inconspicuous (but elegant) new stitches to repair the old. If our efforts are successful it is because the finished product, which is largely new, seems as though it has always been there.

This emphasis on continuity extends to the interior furnishings in the public rooms which were selected with one eye cocked toward heavy-duty performance and the other toward that of appropriate character. The principal public room is conceived as a club lounge for the law students: deep, comfortable, enveloping couches and armchairs covered in red and brown look-likeleather vinyl suggest characteristic Anglo-American club decor; wall sconces, table and floor lamps make atmospheric pools of light. An elaborately patterned orientalstyle carpet completes what we believe to be a familiar and appropriate ensemble.

1

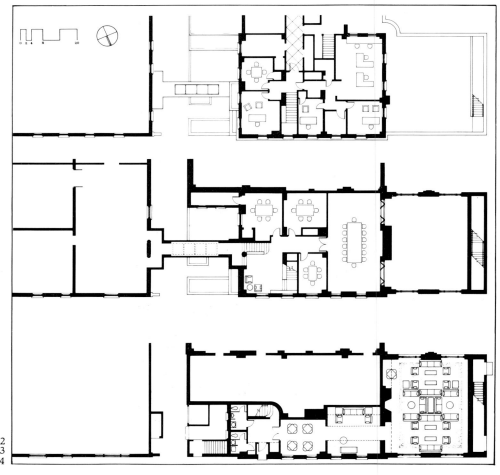

1. Main room looking south
2. Third floor plan
3. Second floor plan
4. First floor plan
5. Interior Elevation
6. Interior view of balcony
7. Entrance
8. Interior wall trim detail
9. View from balcony

2
3
4

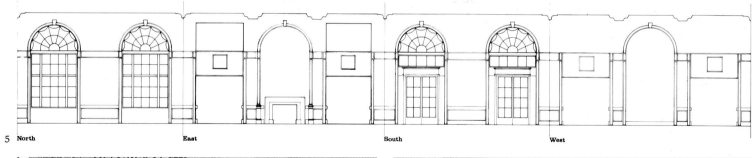

5   North   East   South   West

6

9

7

8

1975-1976 Residence · Long Island · New York

Though technically an alteration, this project might more accurately be described as a re-creation of a 1906 carriage house which had been virtually lost in a fire. Moldings and columns are newly designed in emulation of traditional architectural ornament; the traditional and subtle color scheme reinforces the patterns of the ornamental detail and articulates the lofty cubic proportions of the downstairs rooms. A grand stair hall, like those in the Shingle Style houses of the 1880s, leads to the bedrooms in what was once the hay loft on the second floor. A new screened porch, a pool and pavilions clearly conform to, and expand upon, the vocabulary of the older structure.

1. Pool pavilion
2. Pool pavilion looking south
3. Main house looking north
4. View of addition looking east

3

4

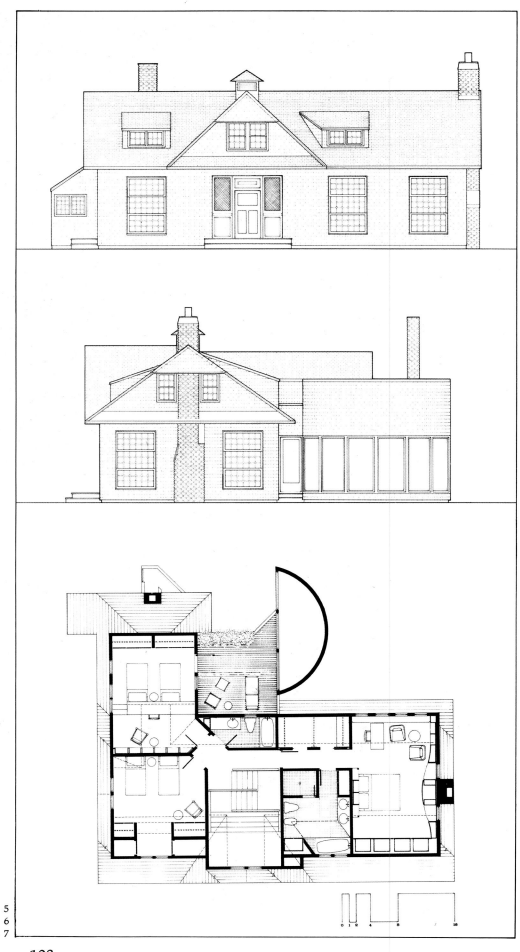

8

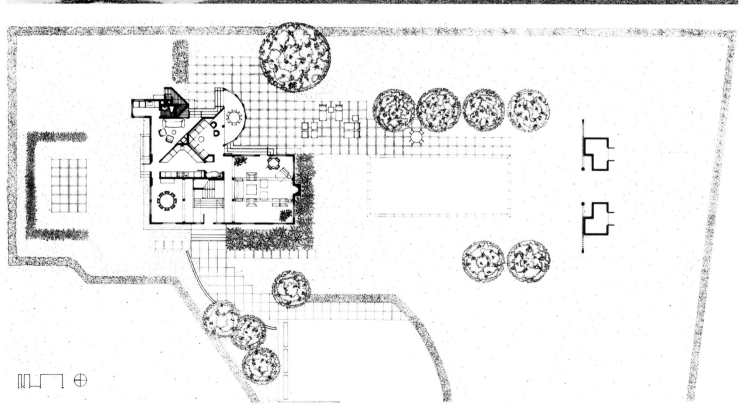

9

5. East elevation
6. South elevation
7. Second floor plan
8. General view of main house
9. Site plan

10. View of stairs looking south
11. Dining room
12. Living room

11

12

Riviera Beach Suburb · Florida

Singer Island has developed as a result of the post World War II boom in Florida real estate into a resort and residential community organized along a vehicular spine. At present, most of its architecture is devoid of symbolic intention: it is watered-down International Style, deriving its only associative connotations from the similarity of its forms to those used in the gloss-glamour resorts of the 1930's and 1940's in Miami, Acapulco and Rio.

The rapid development of Singer Island has tended to inhibit the evolution of local character and a sense of place. In our proposal for Singer Island, methods and strategies are outlined for the evolution of a sense of place unique to the island, and based on imagery integral to its architectural growth and responsive to the problems of scale and speed that the vehicular "strip" involves. Energies are concentrated on the entrance to the Island from the mainland, the shopping strip, and a new plaza at the principal public access to the beach. This plaza acts as a hub of pedestrian activity; located at a critical bend in the state highway, it forms the gateway to the municipal parking lot and the public bathing beach. The symbolic sailfish gate should become a favorite place for photographs, and the raised level of the plaza provides a clear view of the sand and sea from downtown.

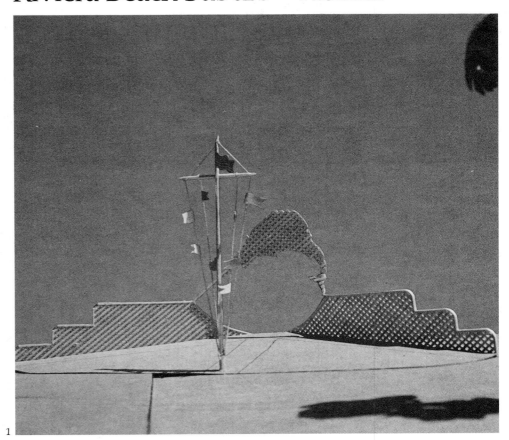

1

1. Model of Sailfish gate
2. Model
3. Model looking south
4. Storefront elevations
5. Storefront elevations

2

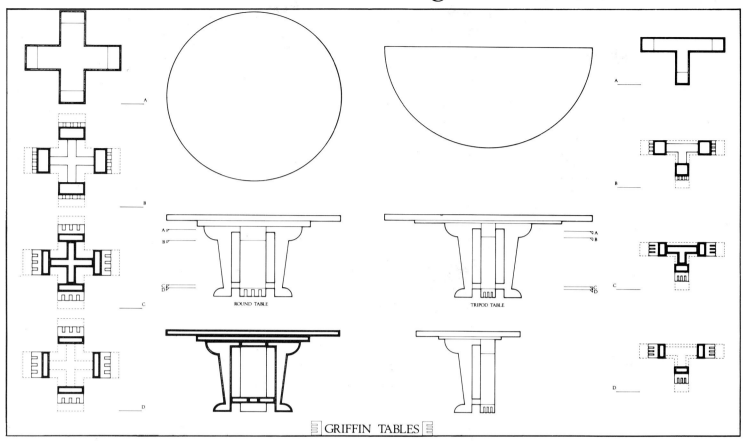

ROUND TABLE

TRIPOD TABLE

GRIFFIN TABLES

1977-1978

Residence · Deal · New Jersey

This house began as a Craftsman cottage, built in about 1910 and notable for its fine woodwork. In the early 1950s an insensitively proportioned addition doubled the size of the house but destroyed its relationship to the lovely garden at the rear. Our task was to make further additions in order to provide sufficient bedrooms for a family with three children, and to establish a new character both inside and out that would respect the original house and obliterate the most awkward aspects of the addition. To this end, certain representational elements of *fin de siecle* design such as the s-curve and the square-doweled stair screen (borrowed from Mackintosh's Glasgow Art School) were combined with heightened representations of traditional elements such as the elaborate treatment of the front door (necessarily located on the side of the house), of the latticed false gable on the garden facade, and of the superimposed scale and Serliana at the fireplace suggesting an inglenook. Taken together, these iconographic elements, even more than the modifications made in the plan and section, give the renovated house the coherent and evocative character it probably had not for a very long time enjoyed.

1. View of entrance looking east
2. Axonometric
3. Rear elevation
4. Staircase
5. Living room looking east

1

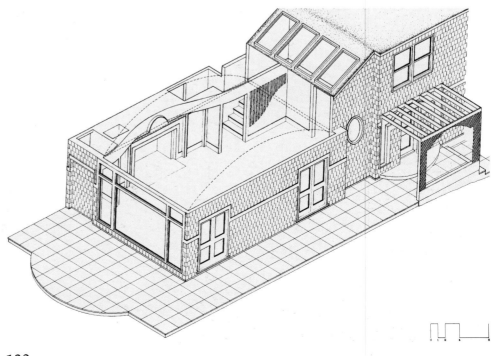

2

3

4

5

1978

Erbun Fabrics Showroom · N.Y.C.

This fabric showroom occupies an awkward space in the Design and Decoration Building. The mirrored lattice walls are arranged like the leaves of a traditional folding screen to create multiple reflections and lead customers past the fabric carousels. Despite the extensive use of mirrors, the lattice and other woodwork give the bounding walls a sense of permanence and scale. The neutral color scheme of white, grey and black complements the colorful fabrics.

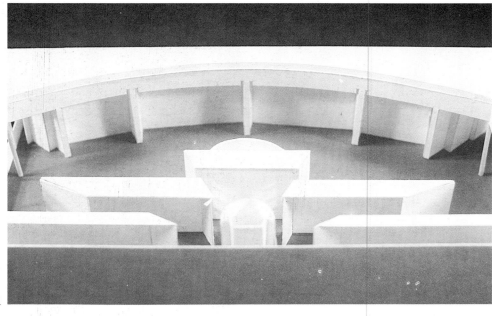

1

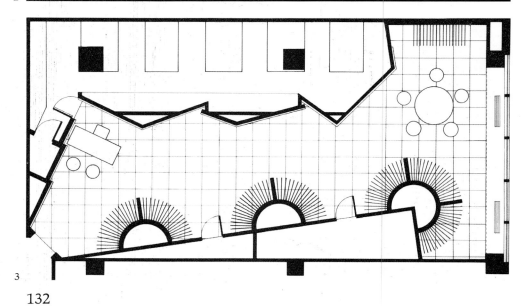

2

1. Model of Scheme two
2. Model of Scheme two
3. Floor plan
4. General view of fabric showroom

3

4

1978

First Avenue Squash Club · N.Y.C.

This small 3-court squash facility occupies space initially intended for twin cinemas in the basement of a recently completed apartment building. A variety of strategies were employed to brighten and lighten the character of the subterranean space without compromising its essential nature as an artificially lit and ventilated environment. Thus, while the stepped profile of the pilasters suggests columns supporting great weight, their comparative thinness and the mirrored ceiling conspire to dematerialize the building mass and suggest a spacious airiness not really there.

Similarly, a game of reversals is played between the club lounge, conceived of as a "veranda" or "terrace" located between the club "house" containing the service desk (set behind the screen wall), and the glass walled squash courts themselves which are intended to be seen as "outside". This allusion to the out-of-doors, and to country club life, is carried further through the use of slate gray carpeting, which evokes bluestone terracing, and sky blue painted walls which are particularly effective as seen reflected in the ceiling.

1. General view of entrance facade
2. General view of lounge and control desk
3. Floor plan

1

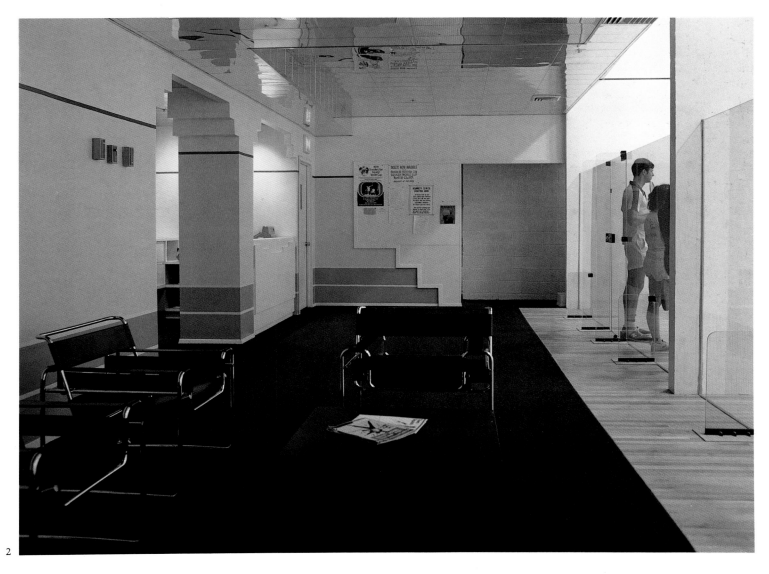

2

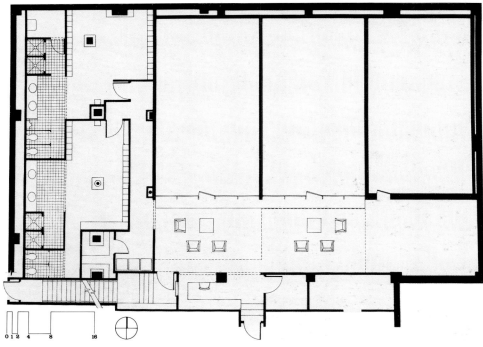

1979

Cottage · East Hampton · New York

The problem here was a daunting one: the amelioration of a small, carpenter-built post-World War II cottage of absolutely no inherent charm. To this end, modest improvements were made to the exterior, most notably the enhancement of the door to the kitchen with an elaborate, classicizing surround executed in plywood. Inside, wooden stripping gives scale to the formerly undifferentiated volume of the living room; with layered plywood again used to emphasize important features such as the fireplace.

1. Entrance
2. General view of house looking west
3. Interior view of living room
4. Ceiling detail

1

2

3

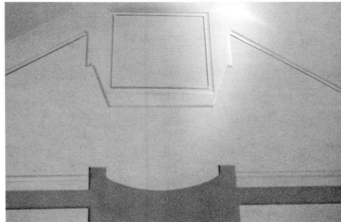

4

1978

Fresh Cafe · New York City

This proposal for a new type of cafe selling light sandwiches, fruit drinks, exotic coffees and fine pastries was to have occupied a store-front in a typically banal speculative apartment building on First Avenue. Color and the highly articulated entrance vestibule are intended to evoke a sub-tropical atmosphere that is associated with citrus groves, jasmine and starry night skies, all combining to reinforce the owner's conception of gastronomic purity and the need to establish a sense of place in an absolutely impersonal context.

1

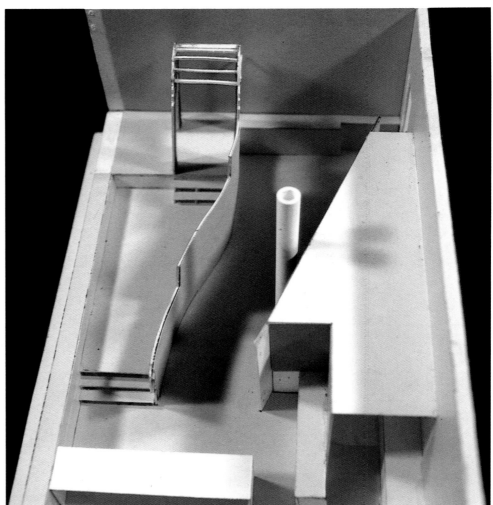

1. Model
2. Model
3. Axonometric

2

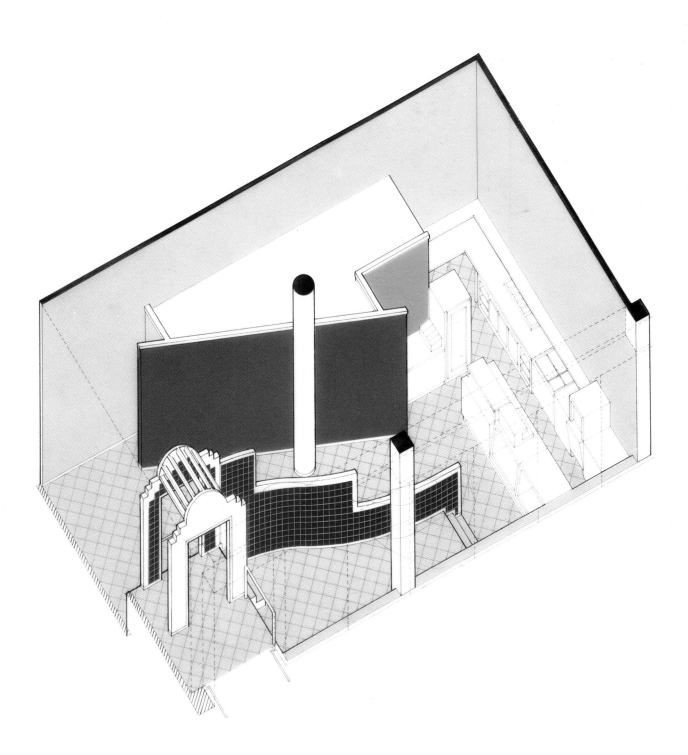

3

1979

Residence · East Hampton · New York

This complex of buildings includes a spacious residence and a separate studio for the owner, a musician and composer. The formal impetus of the scheme comes from the local architectural context—the Shingle Style of the 1880s and 1890s—and from the generic character of suburban estate planning of the early part of this century. The main house employs traditional compositional strategies to produce a suite of rooms across the garden front which are at once discrete and centered yet opened to each other, to the grass terrace, and to the formal garden beyond.

The studio is conceived of as a converted carriage house. The ornamental treatment of the gable ends reflects the shifted center of the double-height work room with respect to the overall composition. The studio is closed on three sides to provide privacy from family activities; on the fourth it opens to a small, walled garden.

1. Aerial view of model looking south
2. Site plan

1

2

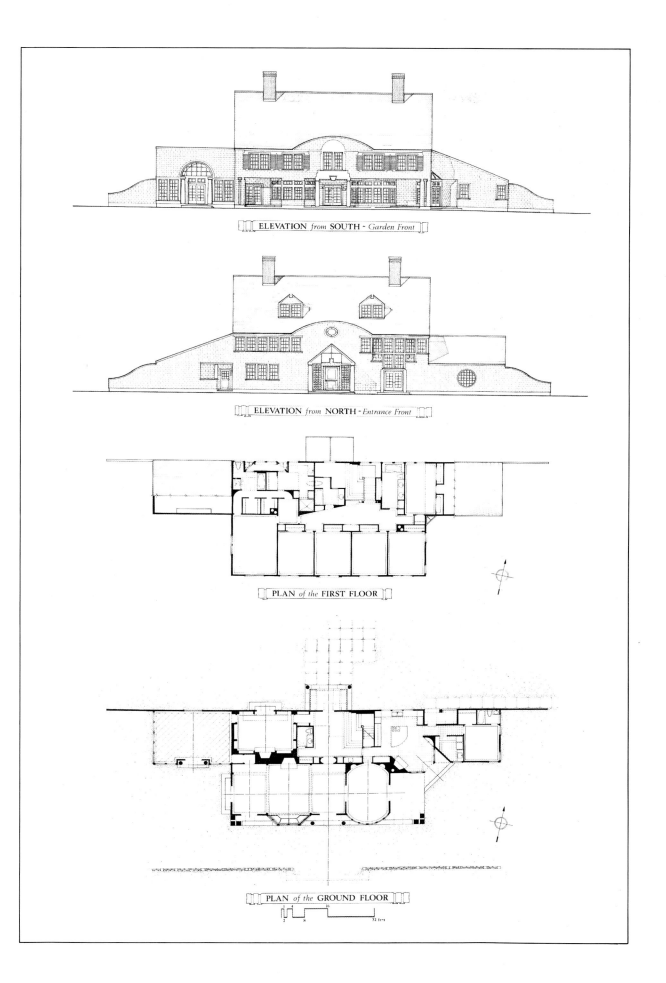

ELEVATION *from* SOUTH ~ *Garden Front*

ELEVATION *from* NORTH ~ *Entrance Front*

PLAN *of the* FIRST FLOOR

PLAN *of the* GROUND FLOOR

3

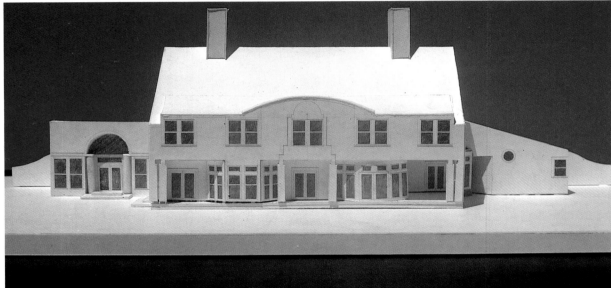

4

5

142

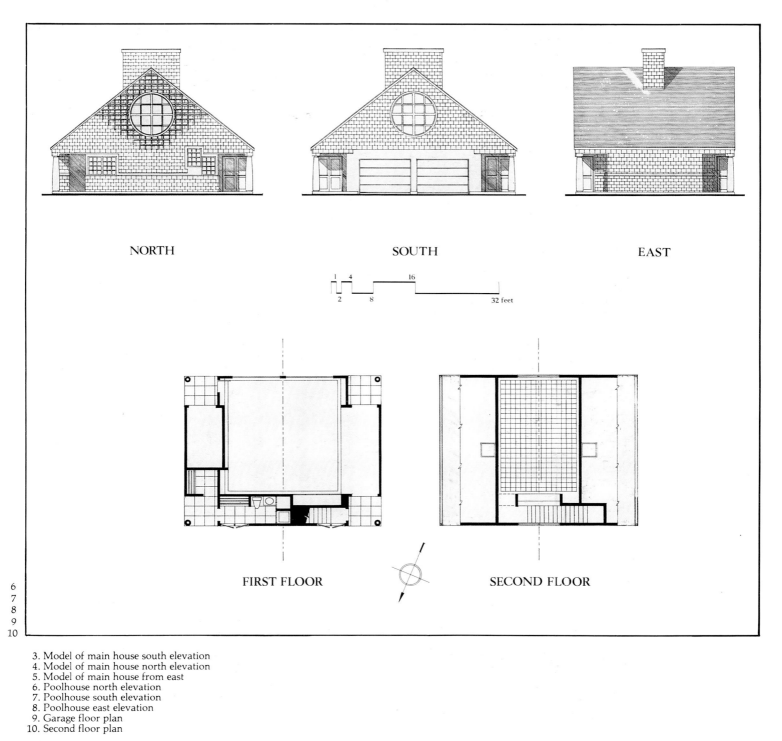

NORTH   SOUTH   EAST

FIRST FLOOR   SECOND FLOOR

3. Model of main house south elevation
4. Model of main house north elevation
5. Model of main house from east
6. Poolhouse north elevation
7. Poolhouse south elevation
8. Poolhouse east elevation
9. Garage floor plan
10. Second floor plan

11

12

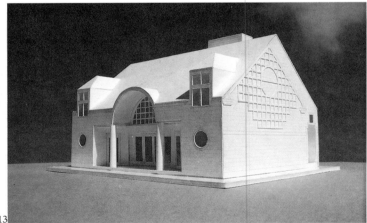

13

14

144

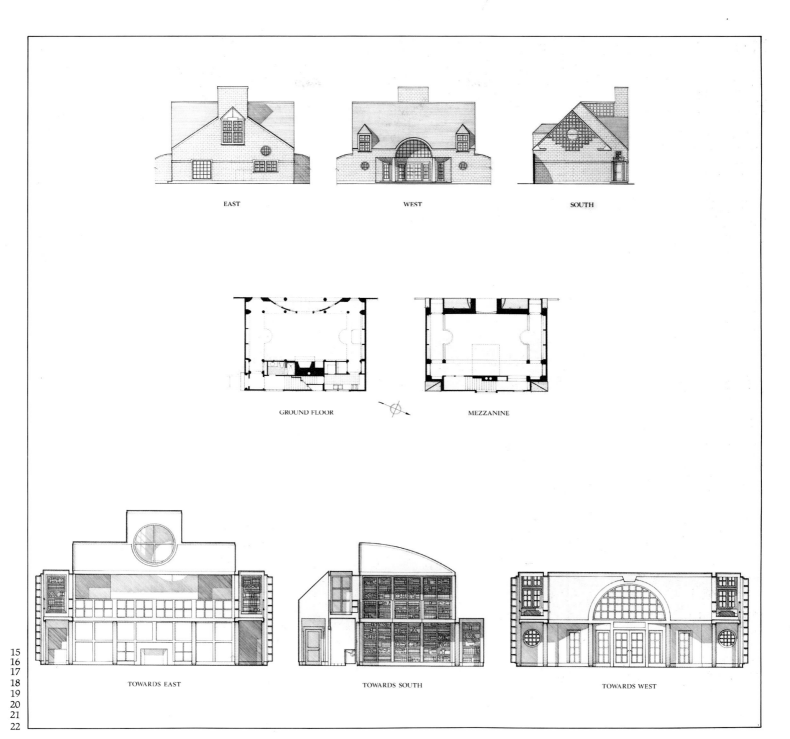

EAST

WEST

SOUTH

GROUND FLOOR

MEZZANINE

TOWARDS EAST

TOWARDS SOUTH

TOWARDS WEST

15
16
17
18
19
20
21
22

11. Model of studio entrance
12. Model of studio
13. Model of studio
14. Model of studio
15. Studio east elevation
16. Studio west elevation
17. Studio south elevation
18. Studio ground floor plan
19. Mezzanine floor plan
20. Studio interior elevation towards east
21. Studio interior elevation towards south
22. Studio interior elevation towards west

1978

Redtop · Dublin · New Hampshire

This superb shingle style house was designed by Peabody and Stearns in 1887. It was expanded at least once by the original architects (who considerably "Georgianized" it) and once by other architects who added on a vast wing for servants. For about 10 years previous to our work, the house was abandoned.

Our task was to remove much of the servants wing (the tail end of which was converted to a garage) and to begin a process of restoration of the decayed building fabric. Most importantly, the removal of the servants' wing necessitated the design of an entire new end to the house, undertaken in the spirit of the original house, with familiar motifs of the Shingle Style restated in relationship to the character and scale of the original house.

1. General view of addition
2. General view of house ca. 1900
3. General view of house entrance ca. 1900
4. General view of house after renovation
5. First floor plan
6. Second floor plan
7. View of renovation under construction
8. Third floor plan

1

2

3

4

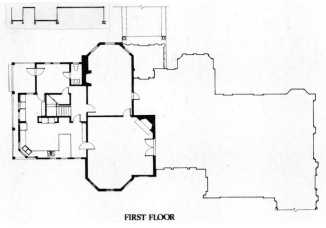

5

FIRST FLOOR

7

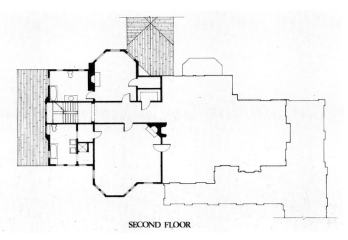

6

SECOND FLOOR

8

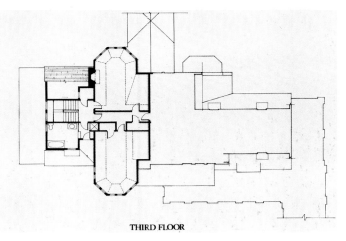

THIRD FLOOR

NORTH

WEST

SOUTH

0 4 8 16 32

148

General view of entrance elevation

Gramercy Park Apartment · N.Y.C.

Located in one of the oldest apartment houses in Manhattan, this design balances the need to accommodate both a growing family in relatively close quarters and the inherent character of the original apartment (which was built in 1882 and renovated around 1900). This scheme reveals a developing repertoire of spatial and ornamental strategies which for contextual reasons seek to extend the language of classicism in relationship to current techniques and sensibilities.

To gain more room in the private part of the apartment and to accommodate the informal life style of the family, the kitchen was relocated behind a large freestanding cabinet wall, designed in emulation of an Edwardian china closet, which screens it from the dining room. A partition at the entrance to the master bedroom creates both a study area and a sense of privacy. Irony is introduced through the use of a negative silhouette column. The cabinets in the children's bedrooms recall the Eastlake furniture that might have been found here in 1895; the complexity of their form gives these small rooms identity and presence.

1. Study voided column wall
2. Exterior wall of study
3. Interior elevation

1

2

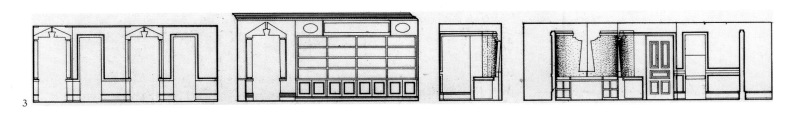

3

4

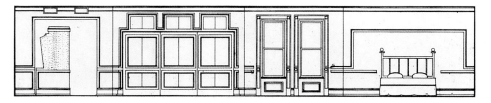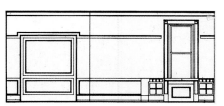

5

6

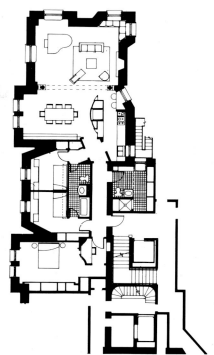

9

4. Kitchen
5. Interior elevation
6. Children's bedroom
7. General view of dining room
8. Interior elevation
9. Floor plan

7

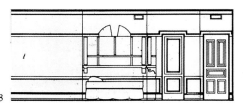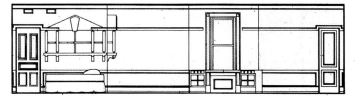

8

International House · New York City

International House is a residence and social facility for 500 foreign and American students enrolled at any one of the universities and academies in New York. Since its construction in 1924, the main building has been renovated several times on a piecemeal basis, often at the expense of the stylistic consistency of its neo-Georgian interiors. By the mid-1950s the altered character of the neighborhood had forced the House to close its principal entrance, which led axially from the building onto a public park, and to open in its place a secure but inconvenient and overly modest doorway at the Claremont Avenue basement level.

Now nearing completion, the first phase of our work attempts to infuse the mundane spaces of the Claremont Avenue entrance with some of the original character of the House's largely unused public rooms. For ease of maintenance and within strict budgetary controls, the older Georgian vocabulary has been abstracted, suggesting to those entering off the street what lies further within. A proposal for the facade of this entrance, awaiting funding, attempts to build up the scale of the tiny doorway and to provide a large sign to identify the hostel to the general community. The use of the canvas canopy is a convenience in inclement weather but also, by virtue of its association with entrances to hotels and apartment houses downtown, contributes to free the House from the negative image of a "dormitory".

The second phase of construction, also nearing completion, deals with the more ceremonial, less heavily used entrance to the House from Riverside Drive. As this area leads directly to the formally intact public rooms, the original detailing has been restored, maintained, and played upon in a quite traditional fashion.

1

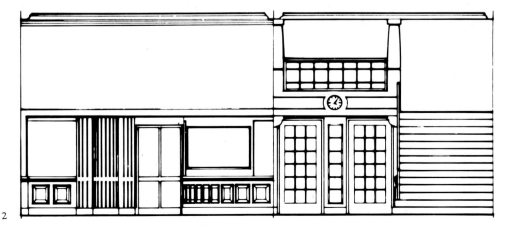

1. Lobby entrance
2. Interior elevation of lobby
3. General view of lobby

2

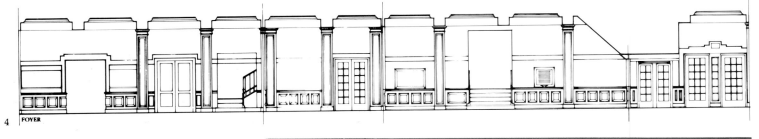

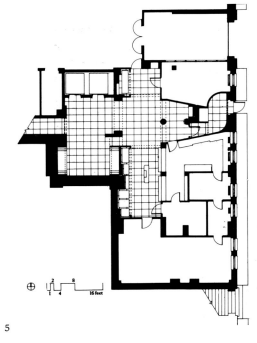

5

6

7

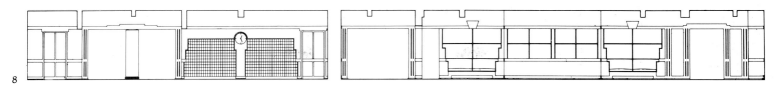

8

9

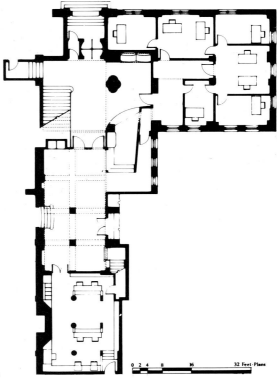

11

10

4. Interior elevations
5. Claremont Avenue lobby floor plan
6. Model of proposed street elevation
7. Model of proposed street elevation
8. Interior elevation of foyer
9. Interior elevation of waiting room
10. View of waiting room
11. Riverside Drive lobby floor plan

1979

Super Spa · Bathing Pavilion

Super Spa was intended to showcase new plumbing fixtures and new ideas about the sybaritic potential of the bathroom in American life. The pavilion functions as an oasis. After ascending to a platform containing a hot tub at its center and flanking sheltered banquettes, one enters a high central room in which a combination tub-shower takes on the characteristics of a baldachino; to the left and right of this are rooms containing sinks and toilets, an exercise room and a chamber in which various climatic conditions can be simulated.

The overall character of the Super Spa is related to fin de siecle Art Nouveau and Viennese Secessionist experiments, the former because of its suggestion of sub-aqueous life, the latter for its progressive classicism employing flat areas of color, often in tile, to render the exterior surfaces grand yet not oppressively monumental.

1. General view of spa
2. Ground floor plan
3. Model
4. Interior view of spa
5. Interior view of spa
6. Entrance elevation
7. Interior view of spa
8. Interior elevation
9. Interior elevation

1

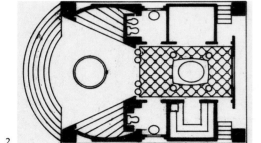

2

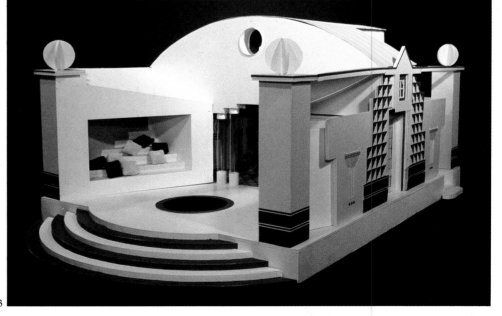

3

4

5

7

6

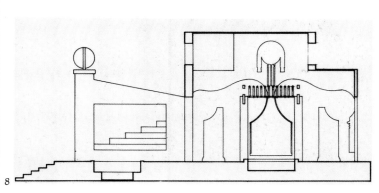

8

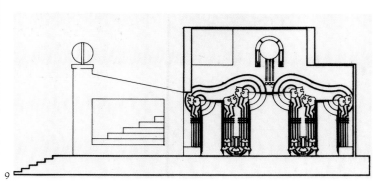

9

1979-1980

Inner Dune Residence · East Hampton

This summer cottage, designed in 1891 by I.H. Green Jr., was one of the early significant summer houses in the Shingle Style to be built in East Hampton. Except for a servants wing added in about 1915 (and removed by the present owners who relocated it elsewhere on the property and converted it into a rental cottage), the house had not been touched and had in fact had only two owners, the original owner and his grandson. Our task was to restore its best features while adapting the house to contemporary circumstances (including heating a portion of it for winter use). Most importantly, it was felt that the house was dreary on the inside: its beautiful wood panelling swallowed quantities of light; and it had almost no relationship with the landscape.

Our strategy was to open the house to the west where a double height garden room was carved out of the building's envelope. Existing windows and columns were rearranged and combined with new ones of a similar character and scale to produce an imposing glazed wall leading to a deck. At the same time the eastern facade was reorganized to provide a central entrance with vestibule and a small dining room which would enjoy light from both east and west. Modest interventions throughout the remainder of the house establish what we believe to be sympathetic and scholarly conversation between the present and its past.

1

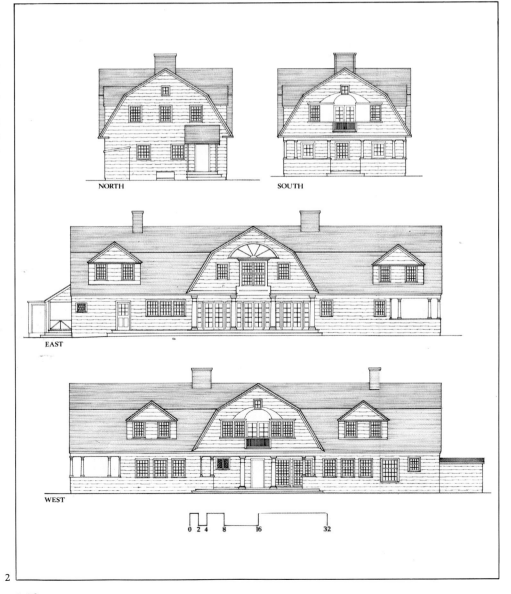

1. General view looking west
2. Elevations
3. General view looking north west
4. Floor plan
5. Interior elevations
6. General view looking south
7. General view of living room
8. Interior view of balcony

2

160

3

6

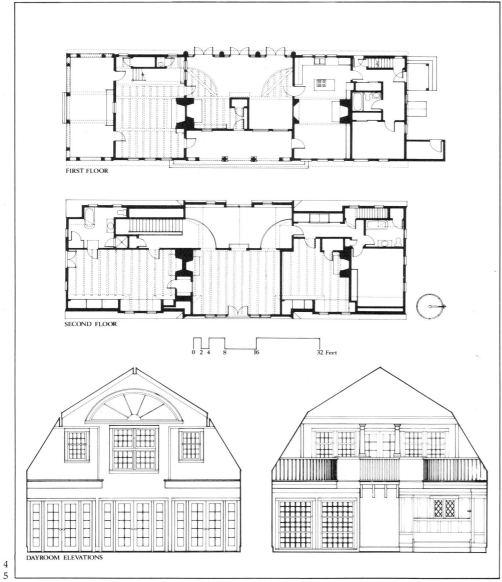

FIRST FLOOR

SECOND FLOOR

0 2 4 8   16   32 Feet

DAYROOM ELEVATIONS

4
5

1979-1981

Residence · Llewellyn Park · New Jersey

This project consists of two components: the renovation of a Georgian house designed in 1929 by Edgar Williams, and alterations to the terraces and garden to accommodate a tennis court and a new structure housing an indoor swimming pool. The renovation of the original structure responds to the owners' needs for more living space and fewer servants' quarters, and to a feeling that the original interiors were pompous in character. In reordering the interiors a syncopated counterpoint emerges between what appears to be, though is not necessarily, old or new. This is particularly vivid on the first floor, where a new yet classically composed columnar order is introduced to counterpoint the free curves of the screen wall enclosing the living room. It can also be seen on the second floor, where a sweeping diagonal of the rusticated book storage wall ties together the principal part of the house with what was formerly the servants' wing.

The pool house is deliberately complex in its formal references—a good-time place cloaked in an envelope that responds to the character of the original house yet which takes on the character of a landscape feature; it is a kind of grotto or nymphaeum that marks a transition between the house, its terraces, and the garden. The palm tree columns supporting the terrace recall John Nash's at the Brighton Pavilion and are used in a way similar to those of Hans Hollein in a travel office in Vienna: to trigger appropriate and pleasant thoughts of sun-filled tropical islands. The tile walls lend the room a subaqueous character. The use of faux-marble pilasters of almost archaic character complements the various high-tech strategies employed to capture solar heat and natural light and to open the pool to the garden.

1. South Elevation
2. Section through poolhouse
3. Poolhouse axonometric
4. Interior elevation
5. Exterior elevation
6. General view of poolhouse
7. Floor plans
8. Site plan

1
2
3
4
5

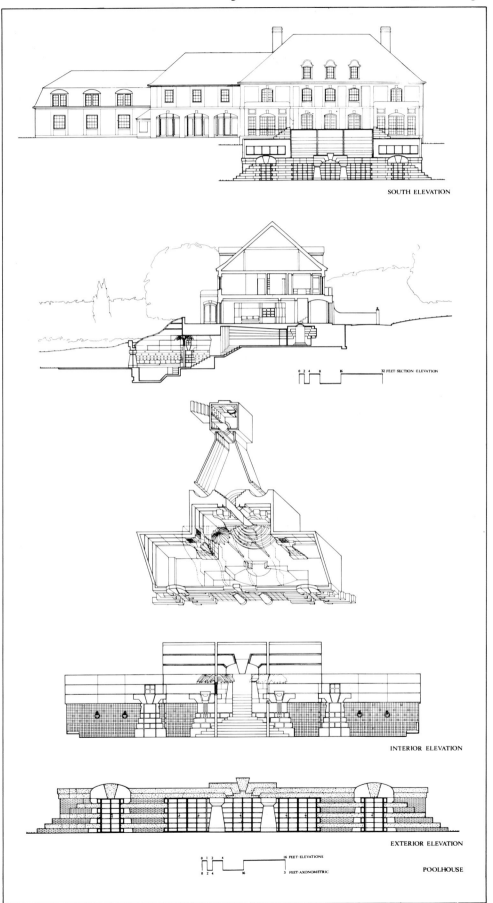

SOUTH ELEVATION

32 FEET·SECTION·ELEVATION

INTERIOR ELEVATION

EXTERIOR ELEVATION

POOLHOUSE

6

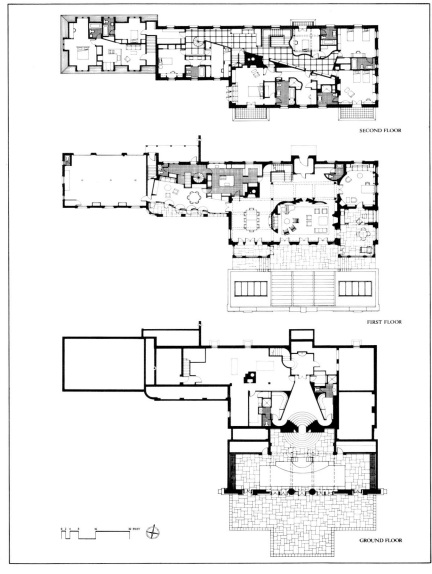

SECOND FLOOR

FIRST FLOOR

7

GROUND FLOOR

32 FEET

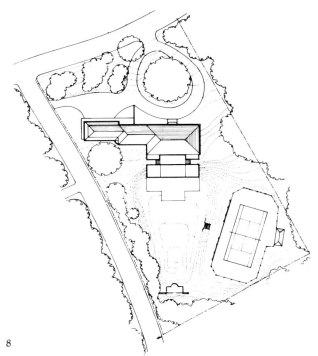

8

9

10

11

12

13

14

9. Family room
10. Dining room
11. Living room breakfront
12. Living room
13. Main house hallway
14. Study

15

16

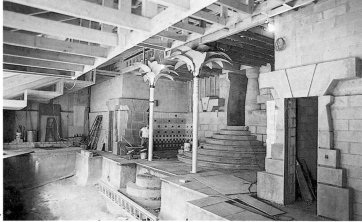

17

18

19

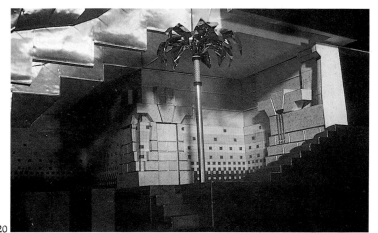

20

168

21

23

22

15. Poolhouse entrance from the main house, under
    construction
16. Poolhouse under construction
17. Poolhouse under construction
18. Poolhouse under construction
19. Palm columns under construction
20. Model view of poolhouse
21. Exterior poolhouse looking south
22. Poolhouse entrance looking south
23. Column

1980   Residence·Chilmark·Martha's Vineyard

Set on one of the highest sites on Martha's Vineyard and commanding views of water in three directions, this shingled house, with its gently hipped gable roof, dormers, bay windows, subsumed porches and inglenook, continues the language of traditional seaside house architecture that emerged in the 1870s and has for many virtually defined pleasant summertime living along the New England shore ever since. At the entrance, the roofline is interrupted by a large gable containing the asymmetrically located front door and a circular window which illuminates the generously proportioned stair behind. On the opposite side, the hipped gables are gently distended to provide a second story balcony overlooking the principal water view.

1. General view looking west
2. View of roof looking south
3. Elevations
4. View of roof look east

1

2

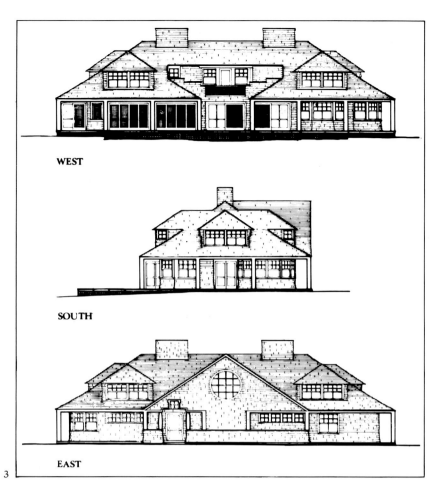

WEST

SOUTH

EAST

3

4

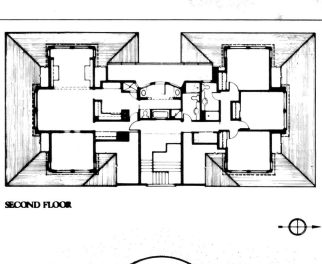

SECOND FLOOR

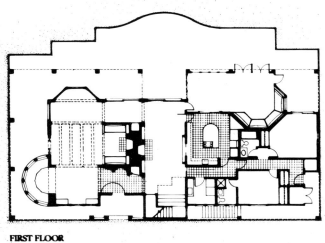

FIRST FLOOR

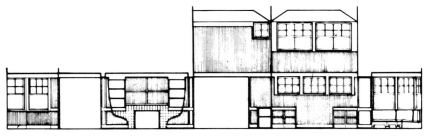

LIVING ROOM

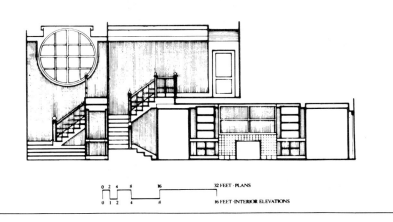

0 2 4   8   16   32 FEET · PLANS

0 1 2   4   8   16 FEET · INTERIOR ELEVATIONS

5. General view looking west
6. West elevation detail under construction
7. Plans and interior elevations

It has been observed that shopping has become a cultural act for many Americans. For this reason, the classical language transforms our catalog showroom into a temple of consumerism. The bold scale of the silhouetted pediment and the stoa-arcade gives the showroom a scale appropriate to the highway. At closer range, column-like cut-outs within the arcade create a scale sympathetic to the parked car and the pedestrian.

The columns, squashed by the great weight of the pediment, record the changes that have taken place in the anatomy of the temple. The stoa-arcade and its heroically scaled metopes are the guardians of the temple treasures. They can also be read as abstracted tables supporting the goods as if in a residential setting. The gold color refers to the sacrificial instruments of archaic rites and the affluence of contemporary American society. The placement of each metope-image corresponds to the approximate location of the product depicted in the showroom; the metopes can also be read from left to right as an idealized cycle of contemporary life. Courtship leads to engagement; marriage and wedding gifts are photographically recorded; the wedding trip gives way to the routine of married life and watching television, while with time childbirth leads to the repetition of the cycle.

The front door penetrates the cycle in the center. The huge void column is related to the scale of the landscape; the column beyond the silhouette is the last vestige of real columns but is made of glass, the material of museum cases, and affords access to affordable treasures within.

1. Detail of entrance facade
2. Cornice detail on front facade
3. Model
4. General view of building from the highway

3

4

5

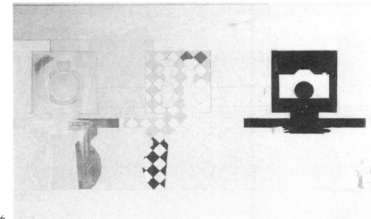

6

7

8

5. Study model
6. Preliminary facade study
7. Preliminary facade study
8. Entrance elevation

1979-1981 Lawson Residence · East Quogue · N.Y.

Set along the ocean beach on a typical, narrow seaside lot, this design seeks to connect with the traditions of the Shingle Style and more particularly with the kinds of "beach cottages" that proliferated along the East Coast in the 1910s and 20s, cottages whose astylar simplicity and direct use of materials surely grew out of the writings and designs of Gustave Stickley. The position of the house at the edge of a high dune made it possible to tuck three small guest bedrooms at grade behind the dune. Thus, the over-scaled stoop leads up to the principal floor just below the level of the dune. It also provides an inviting porch from which to observe the sunset across the bay. The master bedroom is located in the attic, lit by a boldly arched window at the sea side that gives the house big scale and connects it with the high architecture of classicism, just as the eyelid dormer in the master bath pays its respects to Richardson. Though the eroded configuration of the principal floor responds to particular considerations of site, view and solar orientation, the fundamentally symmetrical organization of the mass is intended to give the house a dignity and iconic clarity of its own—an object of calm amidst the helter skelter.

1. General view from the south
2. General view looking from the southeast
3. General view of the main entrance

1

2

3

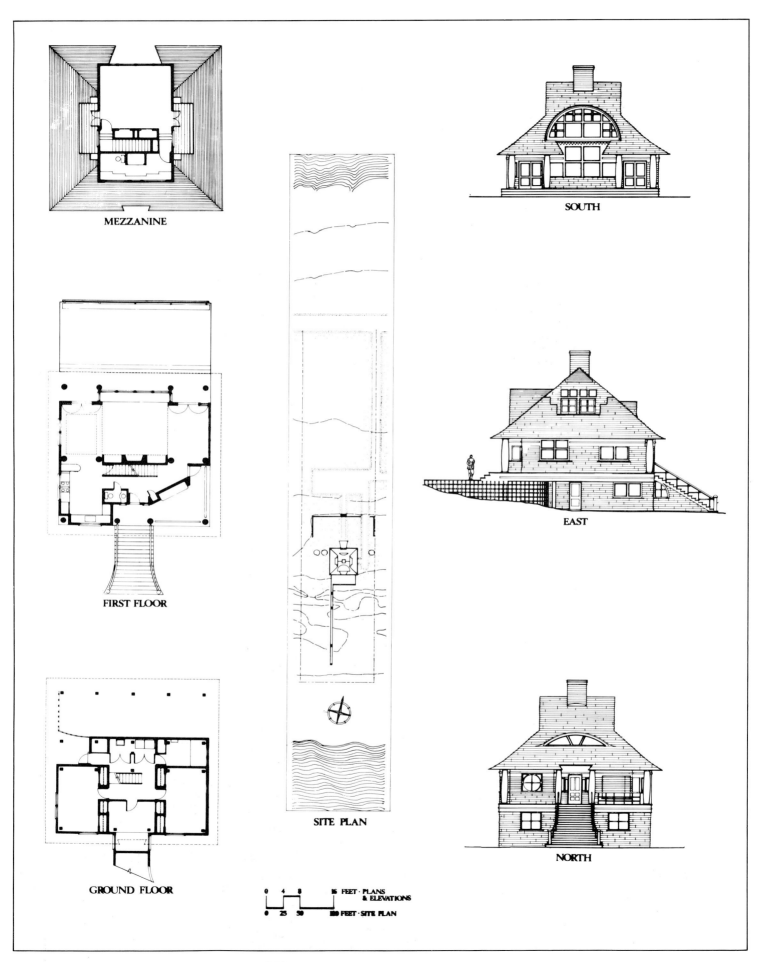

MEZZANINE

FIRST FLOOR

GROUND FLOOR

SITE PLAN

SOUTH

EAST

NORTH

0   4   8   16 FEET · PLANS
                    & ELEVATIONS

0   25   50   100 FEET · SITE PLAN

180

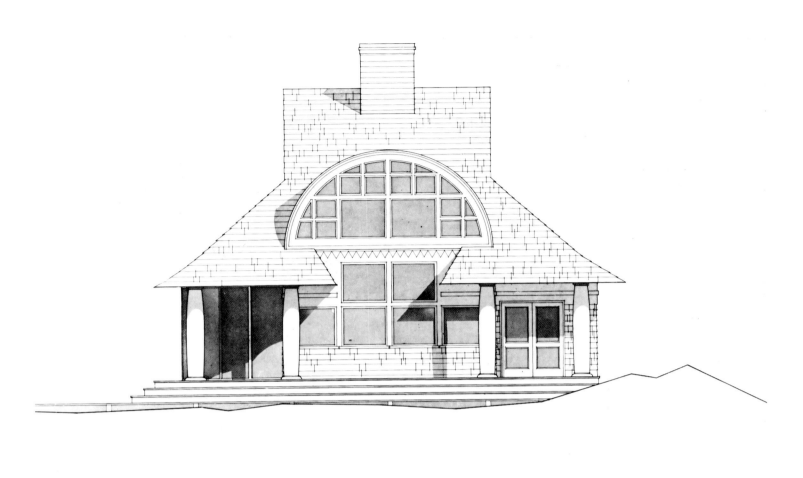

In this modest project—the renovation of a bedroom in a summer house—the tradition of the picturesque garden replete with classical "ruin" is evoked. The headboard cabinet is conceived of as a classical fragment set in a green landscape—in effect both the room itself and the real landscape whose presence is vividly felt through the glass walls.

1. General view of Temple
2. Bed detail

1

2

Prototype Housing

1. Somerset style entrance elevation
2. Wellington style entrance elevation
3. Fairfax style entrance elevation
4. Heathcote style entrance elevation
5. Somerset style floor plan
6. Wellington style floor plan
7. Fairfax style floor plan
8. Heathcote style floor plan

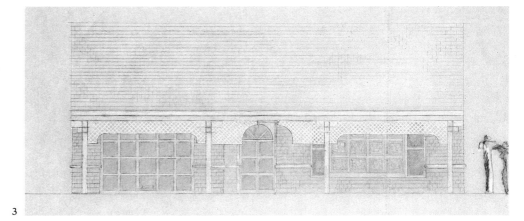

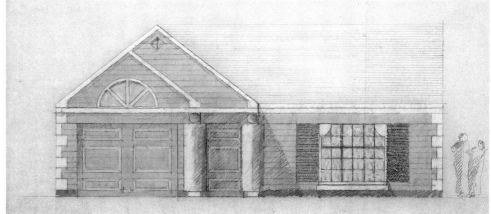

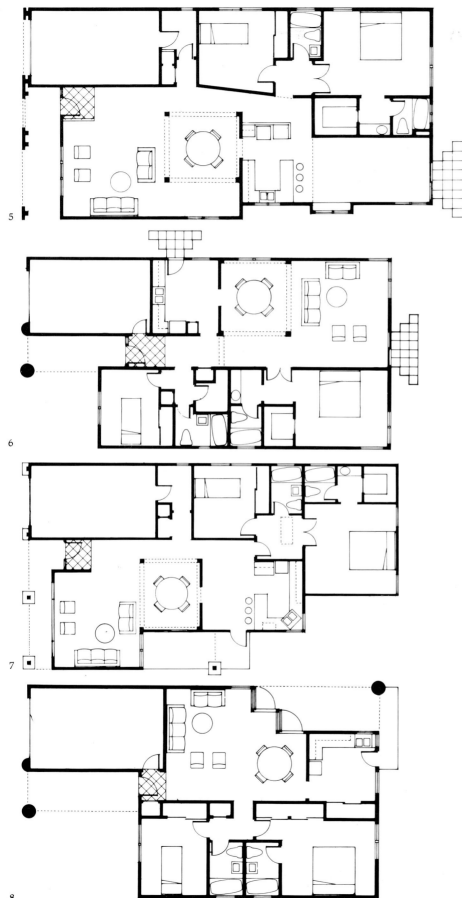

5

6

7

8

1979-1980

Residence · King's Point · New York

This new house in an established residential neighborhood evokes the traditional architectural language of the Regency Style while satisfying the particular demands of site and use. Commissioned by an older couple, the program required good views of the bay from all rooms, ample outdoor spaces for entertaining and a plan which avoided the use of stairs. To satisfy these requirements the house necessarily became long and low. Two symmetrical wings were employed to order the facade and plan, one for the kitchen and garage and another for the two master bedrooms. Two guest bedrooms and the maid's quarters were located on the second floor to give the house scale, modulate the silhouette and achieve a double height section in the living room. The front, with its nearly unpunctured brick walls flanking the entrance court, is a quiet, horizontal facade that orients itself about the large green. On the back the pavilion form of the wings is emphasized, making a more vertical and active composition that gives a sense of place to the various outdoor spaces. Here, the necessity of views dictates a more transparent facade, the bricks and columns parting to make way for a glass and steel skin which weaves its way along the perimeter.

1. Elevations
2. East elevation study
3. West elevation study
4. Study model
5. Study model
6. Entry details
7. Interior views of living room
8. Plans

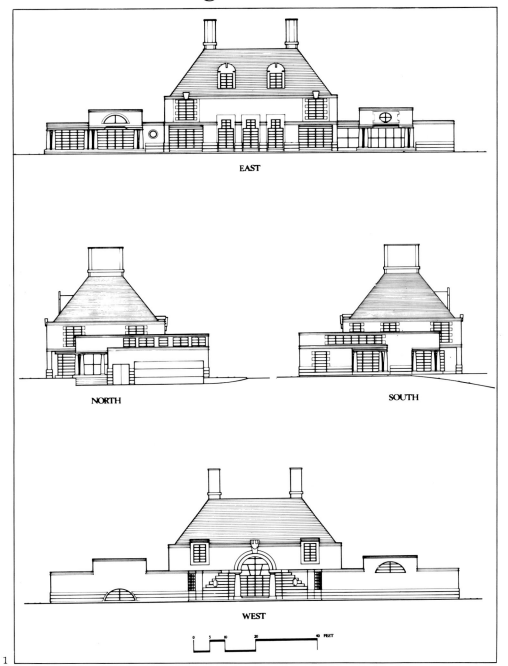

EAST

NORTH

SOUTH

WEST

0 5 10 20 40 FEET

1

2

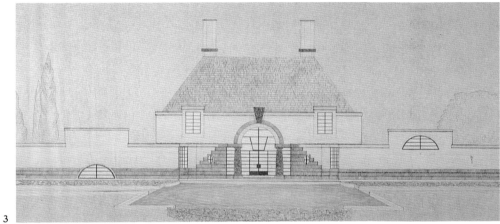

3

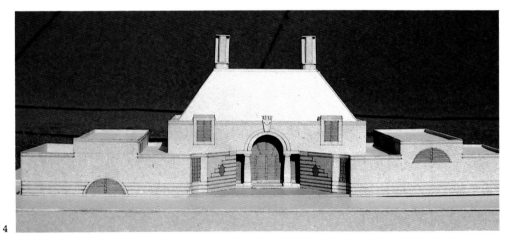

4

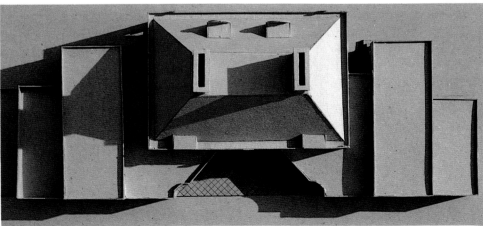

5

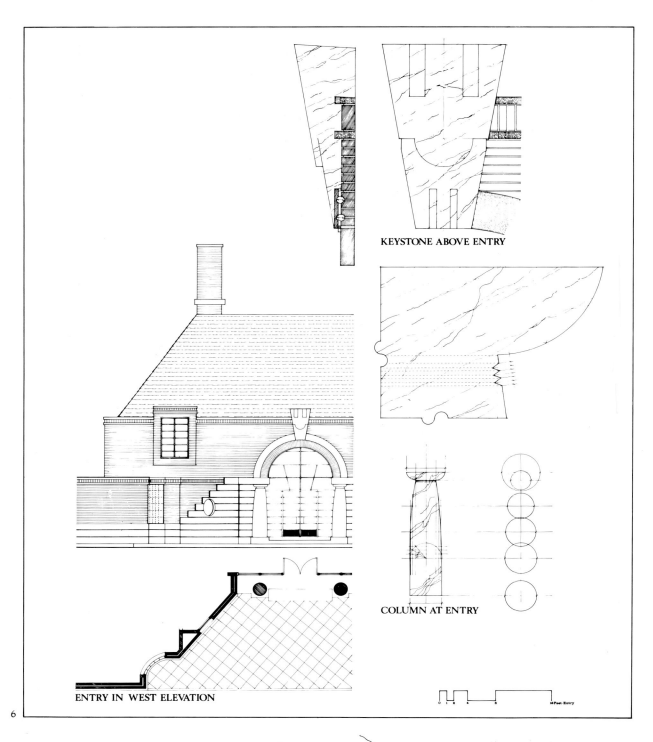

KEYSTONE ABOVE ENTRY

COLUMN AT ENTRY

ENTRY IN WEST ELEVATION

6

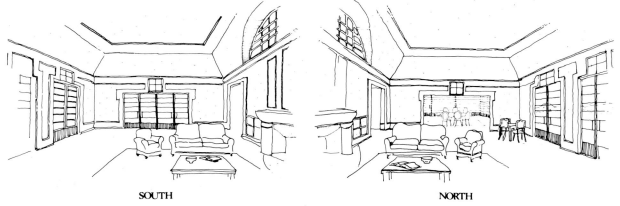

SOUTH

NORTH

7

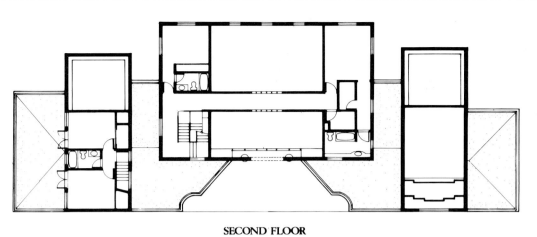

SECOND FLOOR

FIRST FLOOR

0 5 10   20   40 FEET · PLANS

0   20   40   80   160 FEET · SITE PLAN

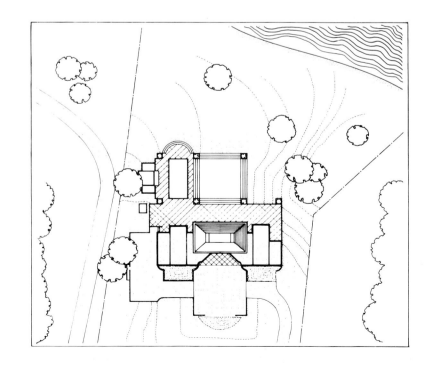

Design Pavilion · Linz · Austria

The central element of the pavilion is a polychromed Greek temple front, an icon representing the recent search into architectural forms of the past. The temple front recalls in a relatively literal manner early Greek temples such as those at Paestrum, Selinus and Segesta, but with the columns rendered as voids, and the spaces between the columns as solids. Since the void columns are the means by which one enters the temple it is as if one walks through history into the past.

The six columns removed from the temple front have a double life; they populate the forecourt as well as the enclosed space within. These columns are humanistic embodiments of architects whose work is of special interest today, whether they are from the past, as outside, or the present, as inside.

In the forecourt is a field of six columns representative of Modern architects from the past. Each is covered with black and white photographs of the work of one of these architects. The columns are arranged to represent a ruin, enhancing the Greek ambience to emphasize the central importance of the classical tradition, and portraying the state of the past after the harsh neglect of Modernism. The upright columns within the temple embody the work of six contemporary architects whose work demonstrates a richness of form achieved through the rediscovery of the past and the conscious attempt to reestablish the continuity of Modern architecture. Illuminated from within to provide the only light in the darkened space, the columns of post modernism are covered with color transparencies of the architects' work and are arranged as if engaged in debate over the issues raised by the pavilion.

1

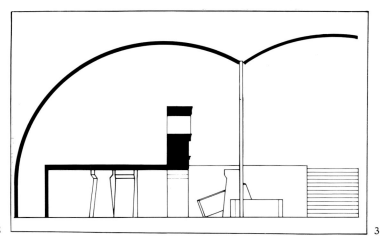

2

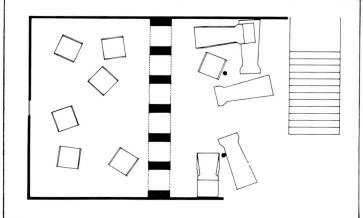

3

4

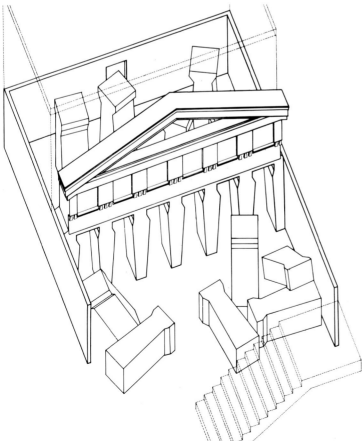

5

6

1. General view of entrance facade
2. Section through pavilion and exhibition area
3. Floor plan
4. Pavilion entrance elevation
5. Axonometric
6. General view of pavilion

Visitor's Center · Shaker Village

The visitor center for Shakertown Kentucky is a building which must fit into a dual context, one of space and one of time. The Shakers planned their town after a model of life. From east to west the buildings were laid out in a progression; dormitories to the east, working, eating and worshipping in the middle and, away from the center of town to the west, the cemetery.

The visitor center is located to the west and since its main function is that of a museum one can in many senses consider it a passage backwards in time. The approach by foot is through the cemetery. One enters the building at grade and, after an orientation lecture, proceeds up through the exhibition spaces, gaining an ever improving view of the town as one becomes more familiar with Shaker life.

The building itself combines elements that are closely based on the Shaker buildings with those that bespeak a spare contemporary utilitarianism, which we believe clearly echoes the Shaker ideals: beautiful materials simply employed to make forms which elegantly express a philosophy as well as a function.

1. Model looking east
2. Aerial view of model looking north
3. Section
4. Elevations
5. First floor plan
6. Second floor plan
7. Third floor plan

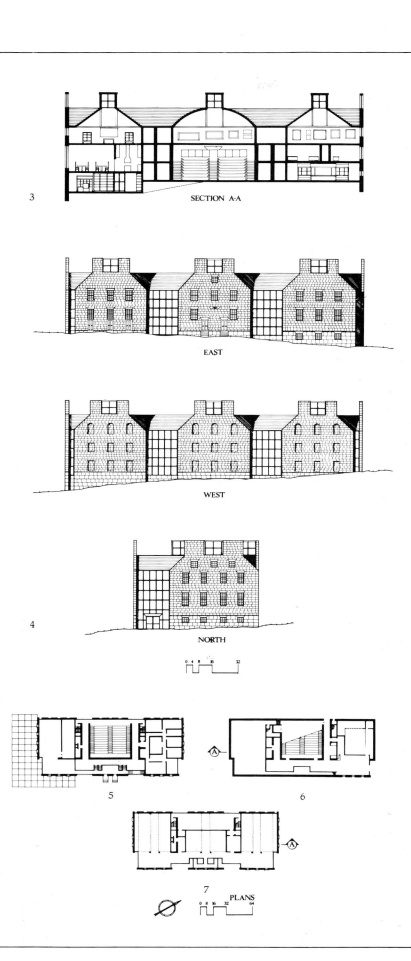

3   SECTION A·A

EAST

WEST

4   NORTH

0 4 8 16   32

5   6

7   PLANS

0 8 16 32   64

The single most positive aspect of contemporary architecture's exploration of traditional values is the recuperation of the concept of the facade. No longer need the facade merely represent aspects of architectural syntax—the building's plan and section—or the processes of its own production. The facade has now been freed to address the public realm with a message of things as they are, and as one might want them to be.

Our proposal for 'La Strada Nuovissima' discusses the reality and illusion of the past—the recent past of our office's work and the distant past of architectural history. Elements of the facade connect these two levels, addressing also the context of the street's ambiguous scale and Venice's maritime past. Thus the abstracted curtain/columns suggest a proscenium to tell not only of a "show" of office work but also of a more enduring drama acted out on a stage of infinite dimensions. While the "show" is a reality in the present, the greater drama is the constantly changing flow of the illusions of different people at different times.

Noble among the players in this shadow play is the Greek temple, an abstraction of which appears as a void on the silent face of a figure standing before the curtain of history. This image inhabits the new street— a Venetian trader attired in gold and red damask before a backdrop of maritime colors. Yet the temple and overscaled moulding of the proscenium refer also to specific moments in our office's stylistic development; the former to the Best Products facade, the latter to the Lang House. On the interior the temple form is used explicitly to frame the exhibit. The threshold is a void rusticated column from Llewellyn Park which suggests the act of engaging the past in order to realize the potential richness of the present.

1. Street elevation
2. Elevation

1

194

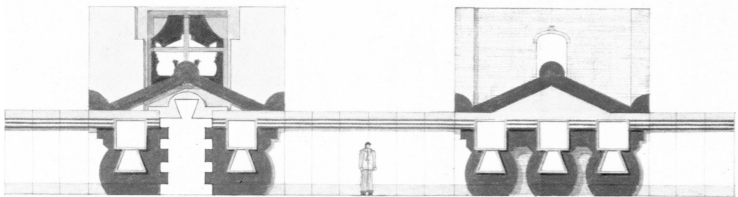

2

3

4

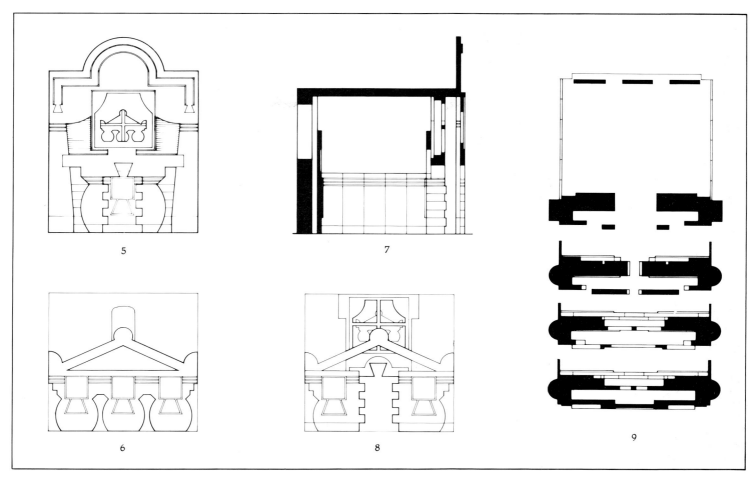

3. Interior window
4. Interior·elevation
5. Interior south elevation
6. Interior north elevation
7. Section through pavilion
8. Street elevation
9. Plan and facade sections
10. Model of street facade

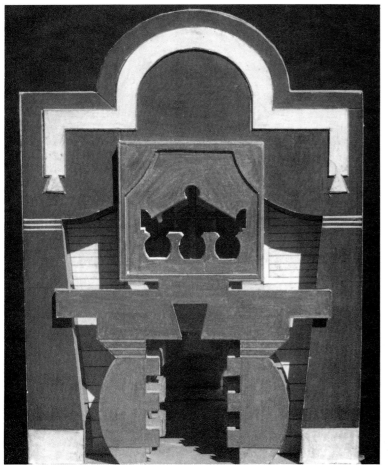

Our project for the new Chicago Tribune Tower takes as its primary reference Adolf Loos' entry in the original 1921-1922 competition, and attempts to marry that project to the Miesian prism. To build a classical tower out of glass, we have used architectural elements rooted in the culture of the past though executed in the technology of the present.

The signboard at the top refers to the cultural conditions of the Mid-West which gave rise to the urbanism of the false front and to the nostalgic name "Chicago Tribune". Our Tuscan order reflects the presumptive moral austerity and rectitude of the ancient Roman tribunes, as does the red and gold color scheme. The signboards also recall Henri Labrouste's "Bridge connecting France and Italy". The word "Tribune" announces that in crossing the river one enters the land where the Chicago Tribune pioneered large scale development, the word 'Chicago' on the north face announces that one will soon be entering the 'real' Chicago of the Loop area—the frame and infill architecture of William Le Baron Jenny beloved by Sigfried Giedion, and leaving behind that other Chicago of suburbs and styles, the cultural complexities of Frank Lloyd Wright, Howard Shaw, and David Adler.

1. Model
2. Historical references
3. General view of tower

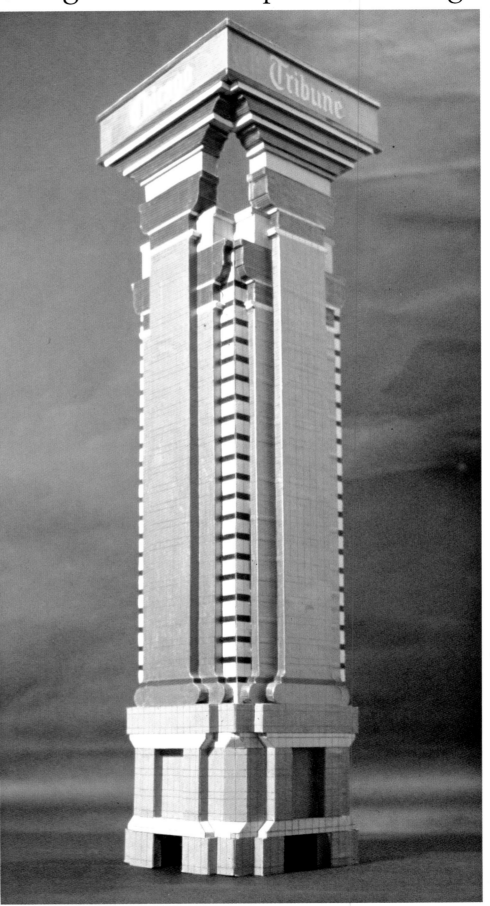

1

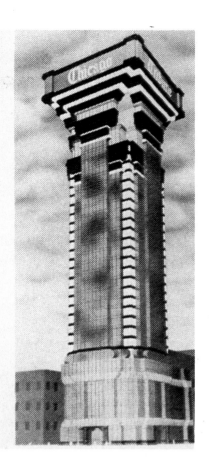

2

3

Classical Duplex Apartment · N.Y.C.

This apartment, located in a landmark building of the 1920s, represents a reconsideration of themes first established in the earlier duplex apartment of 1973-74, whose raw space was comparable. Elements of the earlier design such as the monumentally scaled stair are here restudied in a vocabulary that is enriched by virtue of the use of classical language and by the introduction of a rich and somewhat unorthodox palette of materials that includes a variety of marbles as well as glass block.

The entrance from the elevator leads directly into a vaulted vestibule from which a view of the principal living room can be glimpsed across the stair landing. In the living room, with the permission of the Landmarks Commission, the windows have been lowered and iron balconies projected out beyond the building's edge, at once enriching its facade and establishing a dialogue between the apartment, the park below and the city skyline beyond.

1

1. Entry Archway
2. Entry Ceiling
3. Dining room elevations
4. Lower level floor plan
5. Upper level floor plan
6. General view of dining room

2

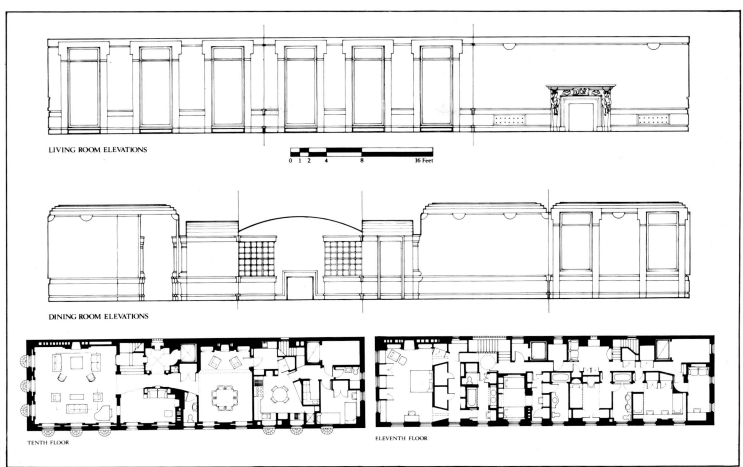

LIVING ROOM ELEVATIONS

0 1 2 4 8 16 Feet

DINING ROOM ELEVATIONS

TENTH FLOOR

ELEVENTH FLOOR

3
4
5

6

7

9

8

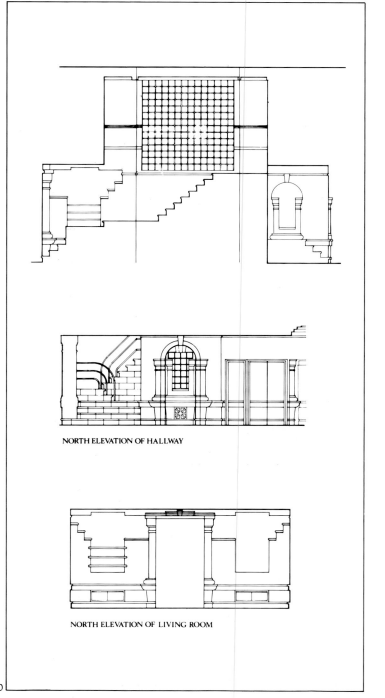

NORTH ELEVATION OF HALLWAY

NORTH ELEVATION OF LIVING ROOM

10

11

13

12

7. Staircase looking north
8. Staircase looking east
9. Staircase
10. Interior elevations
11. Vestibule looking north, under construction
12. Hallway
13. Staircase window

1980

Ferris Booth Hall · Columbia University

New conference rooms have been provided and the individual parlors along the west have been combined to form the Levien lounge, open to the entrance hall and overlooking Broadway, which floods the interior with natural daylight. The conference rooms and the Levien lounge are now complete, as is the principal facility, the Ferris Terrace cafe.

The program for the Cafe was to replace an under-utilized lounge facing the campus with a flexible interior for daytime and evening dining and occasional musical entertainments. Because the room is highly visible from across campus, particularly at night, it was decided to limit the color palette and thereby avoid calling undue attention to the facility. Existing wood panelling was stained black and re-used; the backsplash of the new kitchen servery received a black and white tile pattern. The floor is covered in grey carpet, the tables are black, and the chairs dark red. Existing columns in the cafe and lounge are sheathed in black formica with an applique of white fluting and "capitals" containing high intensity lighting, restating the classical language of the campus in contemporary terms.

1. Column
2. Axonometric
3. First floor plan of Ferris Booth Hall proposed renovation

1

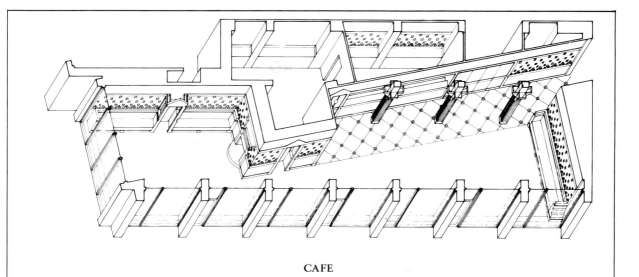

CAFE

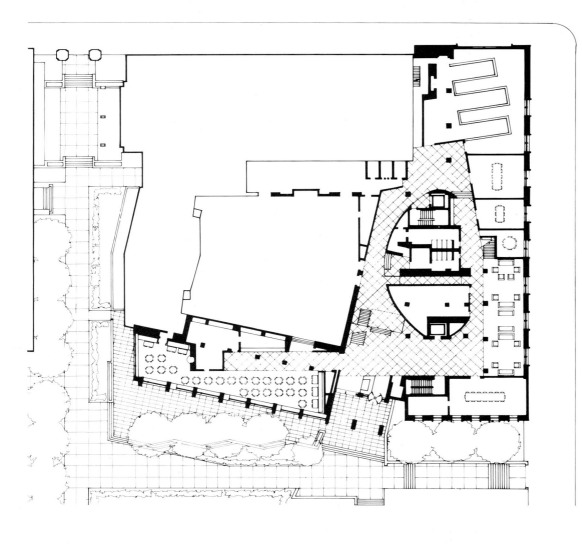

  FERRIS BOOTH HALL
COLUMBIA UNIVERSITY

0 4 16 32Feet

4

5

6

4. Dining room looking south
5. Fireplace looking east
6. Dining room looking west
7. Kitchen entrance

7

1980   City Hall Annex · Cincinnati · Ohio

This project is centrally located at an important city intersection which is as stylistically diverse as it is spatially varied. It functions both as a space directing object and a part of the existing urban fabric. The Annex occupies a sensitive corner site, opposite the imposing City Hall designed in Richardsonian Romanesque style; equally imposing and nationally significant religious buildings occupy the other corners.

The Annex defers to the prominent tower of City Hall while facilitating pedestrian movement between the site and Garfield Place, a nearby park. The detailed development of the curving facade responds to the rhythm of the adjoining buildings while maintaining the scale of the street. Cincinnati's secondary system of pedestrian and service alleys is maintained in the design to articulate the annex into two separate units (the one at mid-block is intended to be rented out to commercial tenants) and to highlight key features of the Plum Street Synagogue across to the south.

The annex aspires to a modest civic grandeur bespeaking its function as a governmental facility frequently used by the citizenry yet not competing with the City Hall which it serves. The building is an attempt to enliven the experience of a particularly rich place in the city; it embodies a confidence in the continuity of historical meaning within a context of contemporary life. The new portions of the Student Annex are intended to respond in a positive way to the diverse architectural styles defining the site and to the very different character and spatial configuration of 117th Street and Sulzberger Plaza. Our response is not based on contrast or separation but on integration; we see our working method as a process of knitting or darning and not one of patchwork.

1

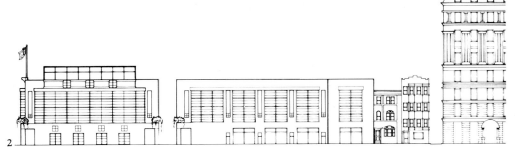

1. View from Garfield Place
2. Eighth Street elevation
3. General view of annex looking northeast
4. Site plan
5. Floor plans

2

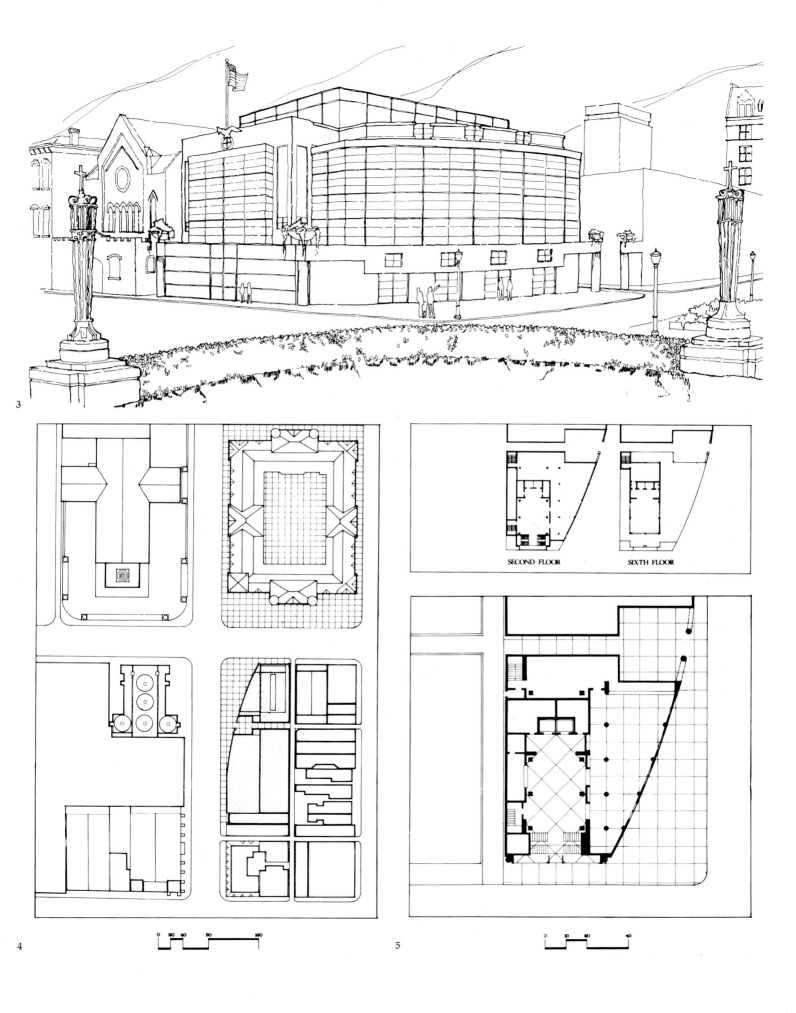

3

4   5

0 20 40   80   180

0 10 20   40

1980-1981

Residence · Farm Neck · Massachusetts

This house is located on a virtually flat site bordered at one edge by high trees, but otherwise open to neighboring house-lots, a golf course and the water beyond. Our design, in response to the vast site and to the particularly complex program, was an archetypal gable form, looking back to McKim, Mead and White's Low House and Grosvenor Atterbury's Swayne House in Shinnecock Hills. The clarity of the gable form lends a big scale which is enhanced by the near symmetry of the principal facade and the pronounced silhouette of the chimneys and dormers. On the entrance side, the projection of a smaller gabled wing serves to imply an entrance court while making the scale more intimate. The projecting bay windows open the interior to the view, while the extensive use of mullioned windows helps to enrich the impact of the vast site from within by framing it.

LIVING ROOM

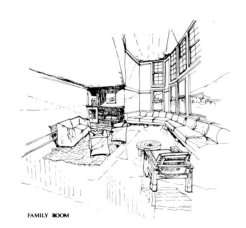

FAMILY ROOM

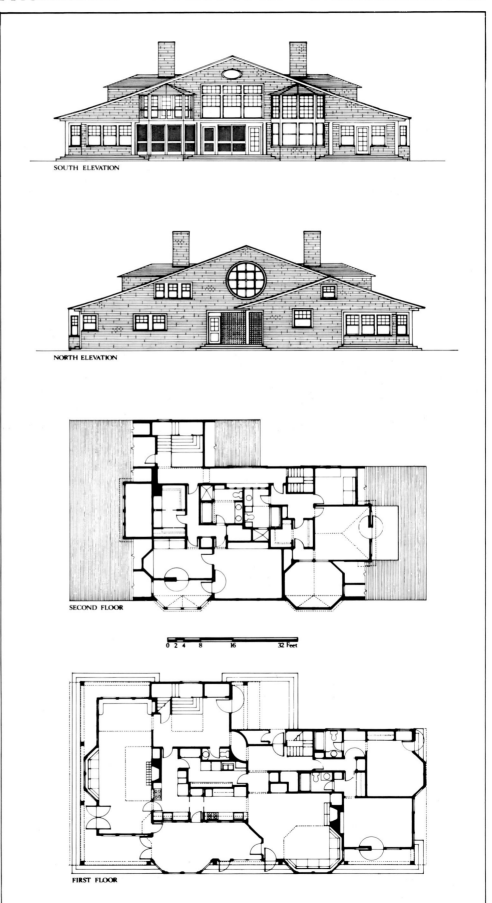

SOUTH ELEVATION

NORTH ELEVATION

SECOND FLOOR

0 2 4 8   16   32 Feet

FIRST FLOOR

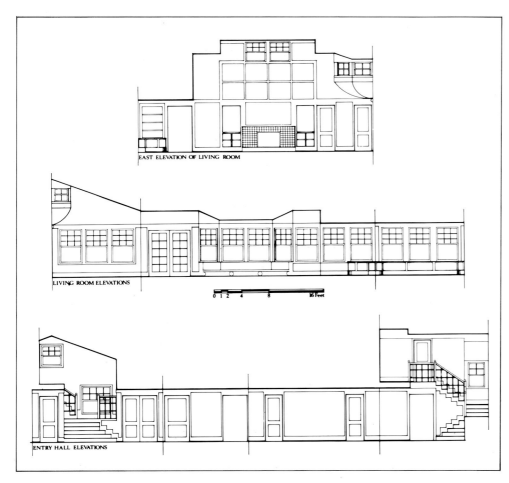

EAST ELEVATION OF LIVING ROOM

LIVING ROOM ELEVATIONS

0 1 2 4 8 16 Feet

ENTRY HALL ELEVATIONS

Garibaldi Meucci Museum Competition

The primary concern in this project is to maintain the character of the existing house, where the Italian patriot Giuseppe Garibaldi lived for several years, as did Antonio Meucci, the true inventor of the telephone, and yet add a large amount of space to serve as a museum of Italian-American culture. It was our concern that the spirit of the place with its informally landscaped front yard and its Gothic revival simplicity not be overwhelmed by a new building unrelated in style or intention.

Most of the building is below grade, the roof forming a series of terraces to display statues and artifacts which are at present rather randomly placed around the site. The stepping of the terraces allows variation in the section of the new museum space. The porch and arbor at the back provide shelter for outdoor activities while screening from view the house on the adjoining property. The terrace is also designed to take advantage of the large trees and eliptical pond in the park next door.

A small pavillion at the front echoes the style of the existing house while providing entry control, a guard house and a connection between museum and terrace levels.

1. East elevation
2. North elevation
3. Section
4. Plan
5. Hall of Fame
6. Entry
7. General view
8. Site plan

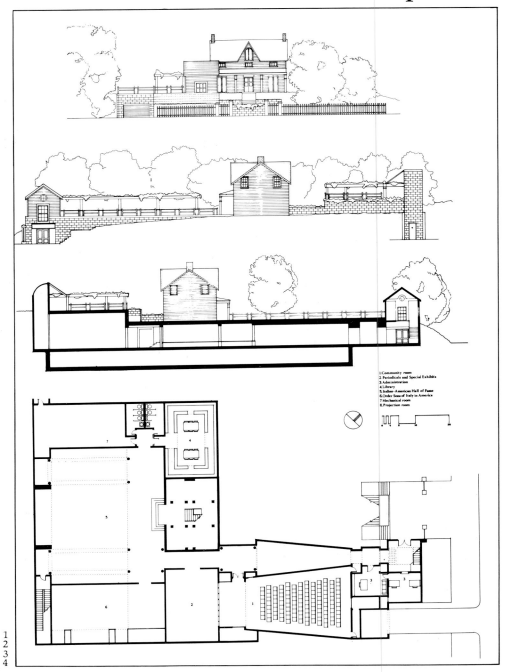

1 Community room
2 Periodicals and Special Exhibits
3 Administration
4 Library
5 Italian-American Hall of Fame
6 Order Sons of Italy in America
7 Mechanical room
8 Projection room

5   6

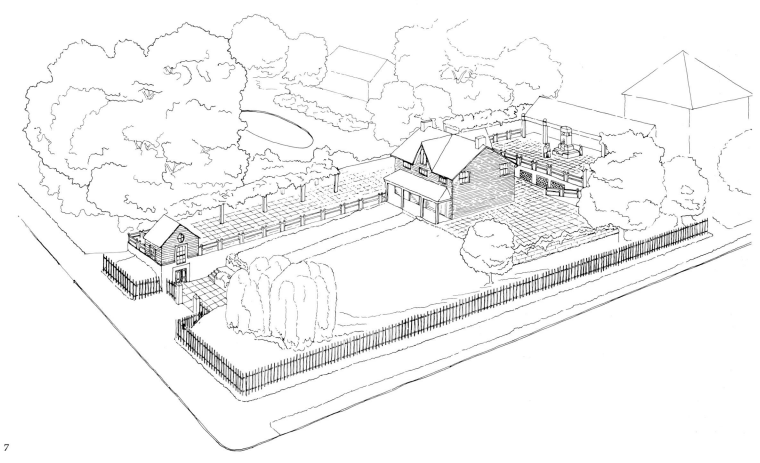

7

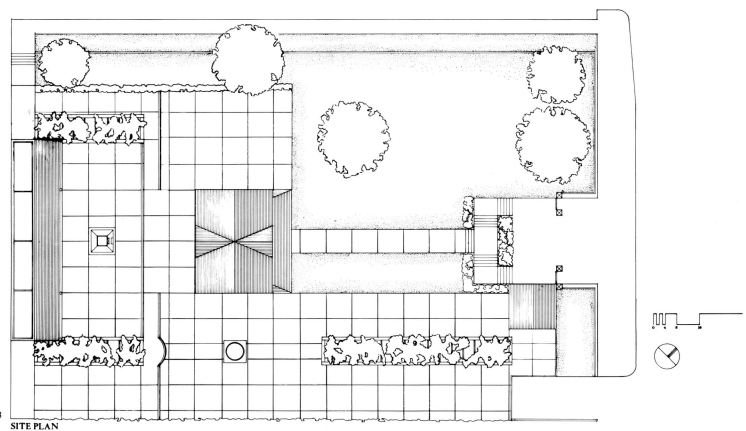

8

SITE PLAN

1980

Collaboration · With Robert Graham

Our collaboration attempts a rich and meaningful allegory for the current condition in the arts, recuperating traditional forms in order to surmount the impasse of late modernist anti-symbolism, extreme abstraction, and reductionism.

The female figure is cast in bronze; the naturalistic modelling reflects our continued confidence in the expressive capacity of the Western humanistic tradition. The figure stands on an Ionic column and plinth executed in faux marble. Further investigation reveals that the column and base are only partially modelled and seemingly emerge from an asymmetrically composed, scaleless mass sheathed in mirror glass, an evocation of the typical highrise office block. The contrast between the two systems of composition in the base—the classicist and the modernist—is an explicit representation of the disjunction currently characteristic of the arts in general, and architecture in particular.

The triumph of mechanomorphology over humanism, long and impatiently awaited by the purveyors of the modern movement, has not come to pass, while its iconoclastic impact as something "new", free of history and style, has diminished with the years. The "new" has become old, or at least traditional, and pre-modernist modes of perception have merely been eclipsed, not transcended. Modernism and classicism now co-exist in uneasy proximity, no longer colliding as opposites but struggling towards a new synthesis.

1. Model
2. Model
3. Elevation
4. Plan and section

1

214

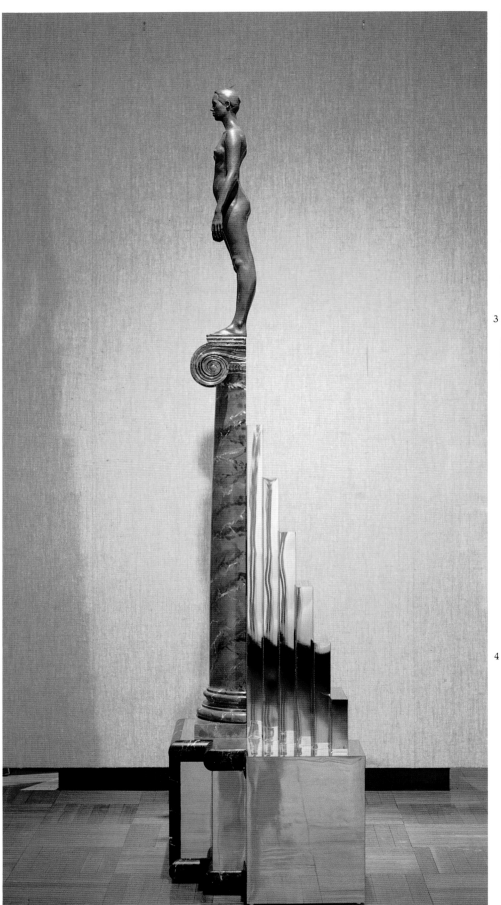

2

3

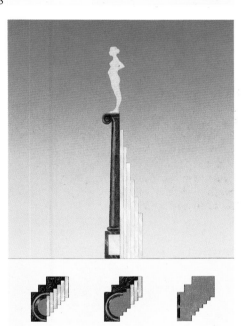

4

Our proposal intends to be a jewel and a strong box at once, a building of diamond-like objectivity set apart from the rough industrial landscape, a working monument which incorporates in metal and reflective glass those qualities of precision associated with the products of the DOM corporation.

The proposal consists of an office tower sitting on a base, which houses the entrance hall, cafeteria and training facilities. The base relates in height to the low mass of the adjacent factory; its shape, that of two superimposed squares set at a diagonal to one another, enhances the frontality of the tower on its entrance side while permitting it to be read more sculpturally from the highway. The tower and the base are sheathed in tinted glass; the colors green, black and silver are selected to further enhance the image of cool mechanical perfection.

While the design seeks to be forward looking in its precise use of advanced construction technology, it also draws on a rich tradition of modern classicism to place itself within a broad cultural and architectural context. Thus the design continues and expands upon the tradition of technically advanced and classically composed buildings established by Otto Wagner, Gropius and Meyer. In its interior spaces the headquarters draws on lessons from the commercial buildings of Frank Lloyd Wright, specifically invoking his Johnson Wax Headquarters in the great reception hall/product presentation room at the top, a room that could become a major public space for DOM.

The tower is designed to be impressive by day and by night. Its principal feature is the stepped dome which admits natural daylight to the product presentation room and, when artificially illuminated, acts as a symbolic beacon blazing across the night sky an image of the DOM company.

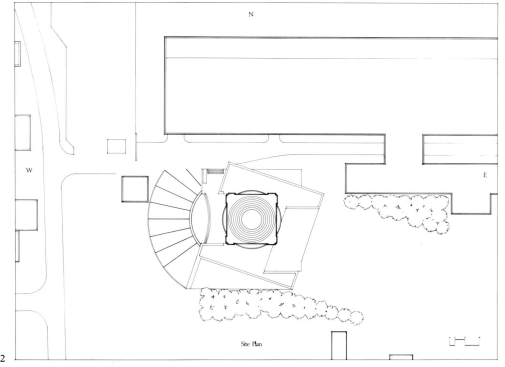

1

Site Plan

2

1. Model
2. Site plan
3. West elevation
4. Section
5. Ground floor plan
6. Typical plan, office floor

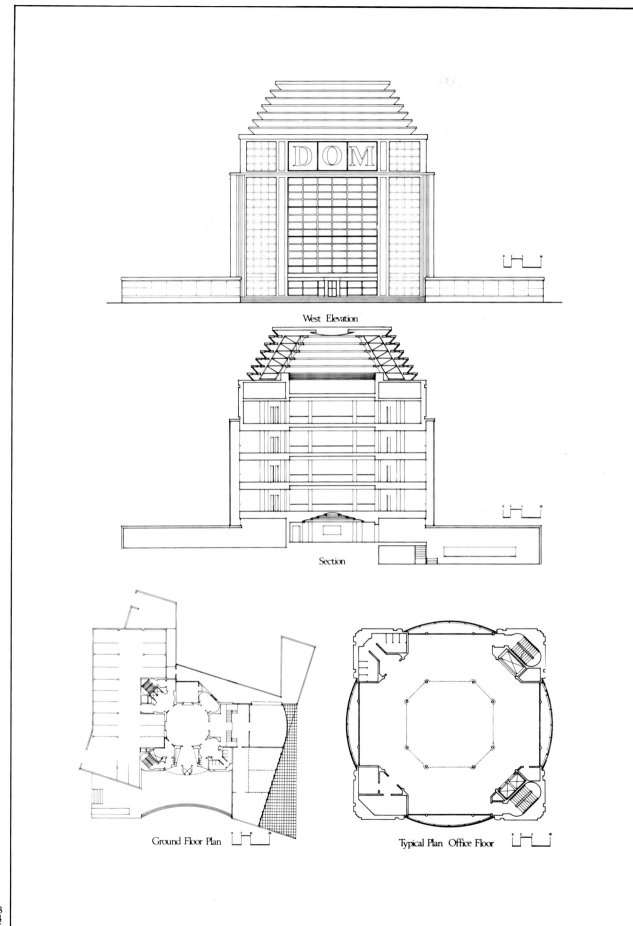

West Elevation

Section

Ground Floor Plan

Typical Plan Office Floor

218

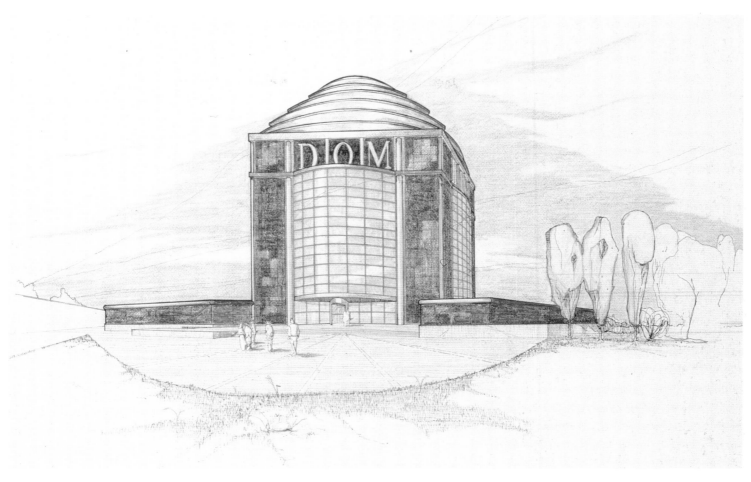

Residence · East Hampton · New York

This house, now being built on a site in the heart of the traditional "Summer Colony", takes its cues from the many imposing "cottages" in the Shingle Style which constitutes the dominant building type in the neighborhood. The site, a former side garden for another house, contains established perimeter planting as well as a guest house and a swimming pool surrounded by thick planting. Our house is located near to the street to enhance the privacy of the garden. The house turns a slender and relatively closed facade to the south to ensure privacy from an adjacent "cottage" that is rather close to the property line. In plan, massing, and detail, the house is intended as a contemporary essay in the Shingle Style. It is raised on brick base, which forms the floor of the screened porches as well as the covered terrace outside the living room. A somewhat unorthodox feature is the chamfered turret of the dining porch which will admit light and air at its top.

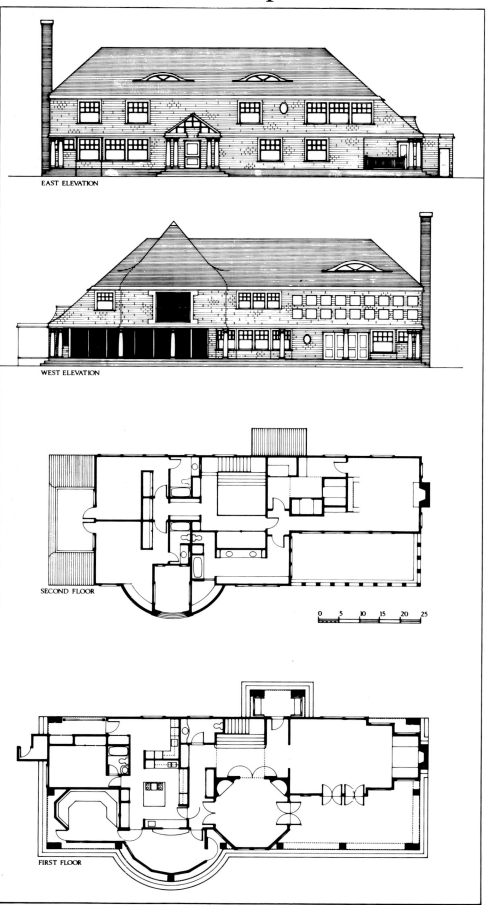

EAST ELEVATION

WEST ELEVATION

SECOND FLOOR

0   5   10   15   20   25

FIRST FLOOR

SECTION THROUGH TOWER

ELEVATION OF TOWER

NORTH ELEVATION OF HOUSE

0   5   10   15   20
0   5   10

ELEVATION AND SECTION OF SCREEN WALL

SECTION OF TOWER WALL

Model

LIVING ROOM

DINING ROOM

ENTRY HALL

BACK PORCH

Young-Hoffman Exhibition · Chicago

1. Model stand
2. Model stand
3. Wall column and sconce

2

3

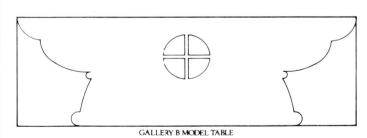

GALLERY B MODEL TABLE

1980-1981

Residence · Locust Valley · New York

This house was to have been built on a large lot at the edge of a former estate which has been subdivided. The intention was to produce a relatively compact residence (largely on one floor) which would capture the qualities of the owner's present, much larger Georgian house designed in 1928 by Peabody, Wilson and Brown. Our design proposed to emphasize the principal living spaces by placing them in a pavilion surmounted by a hipped roof which is flanked by bedrooms and service rooms treated as thickened garden walls. The severe entrance facade on the north leads into a vestibule illuminated from a dormer high above and thence to a broad foyer. The living and dining rooms are one, yet articulated by changes in ceiling height and with columns; the vaulted central bay borrows light over the fireplace from the toplit billiard room above, while a continuously glazed wall toward the garden provides general illumination and inflects the plan toward the best view.

Unfortunately, the best view was none too wonderful, causing the owners' to abandon the project and to buy a more beautiful property facing the water, a property with a house on it, which we are now in the course of remodeling.

1. Perspective
2. Model of west elevation
3. Axonometric of columns on west elevation
4. Section at west elevation

1

2

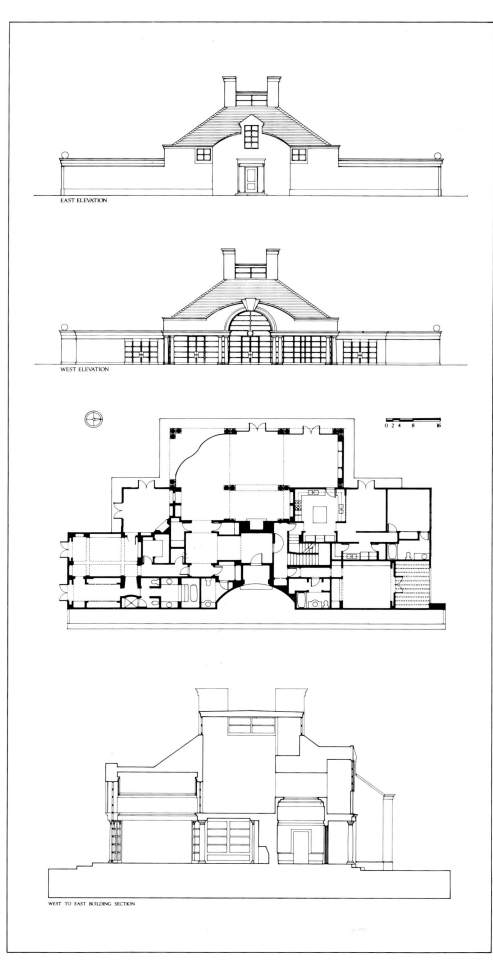

EAST ELEVATION

WEST ELEVATION

0 2 4 8 16

WEST TO EAST BUILDING SECTION

3

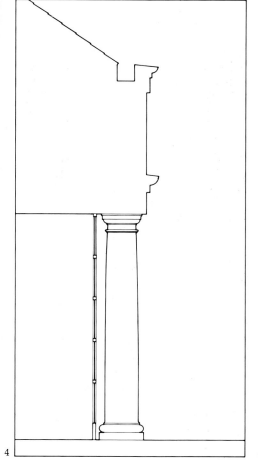

4

1981

Richmond Centre · Richmond · Virginia

This proposal, suggesting a multi-pronged approach toward the revitalization of Richmond's downtown shopping core, includes as its principal features a new 250,000 square foot department store, an equivalent amount of satellite retail space, new hotels, and parking structures. These components are linked by glazed galerias and sky-bridges across Broad Street which tie new and existing components of the Richmond Centre development together and connect them to adjacent convention and sports facilities. From the standpoint of the retailing industry, the principal feature of Richmond Centre is the new multi-function building at the south, which we have called the Market. This facility incorporates all the new retail space organized on five levels, linked by escalators and elevators to three storeys of parking for 850 cars (to supplement available parking at the Coliseum). Two features lend a special excitement to the market; one, a high atrium at the south end, acts as a magnet attracting workers from the central office district near the river, shoppers from within the retail facilities, and travellers staying at the hotels. The other, the Galleria, provides the Market with its bold silhouette and connects it to existing department stores and shopping along Broad Street. The glass roofed Galleria covers Grace and 6th streets, visually interrupting the monotonous city grid while permitting the unimpeded flow of pedestrians. The bold silhouette of the Market structure establishes an image for the entire Richmond Centre and calls the attention of motorists on the riverfront expressway to the existence of the retail core, thereby lending the new development some of the same magnetism characteristic of its rival suburban malls.

1

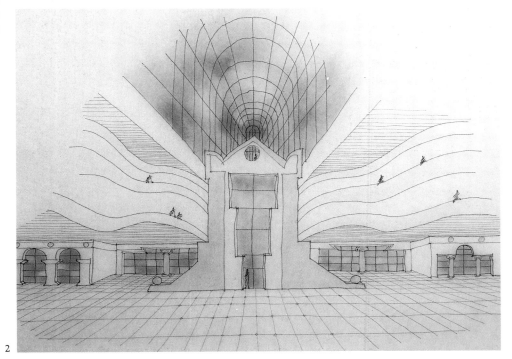

1. Model of complex
2. Interior perspective of shopping center.
3. Perspective of main tower
4. Shopping center
5. Entrance elevation to shopping center
6. Plans

2

3

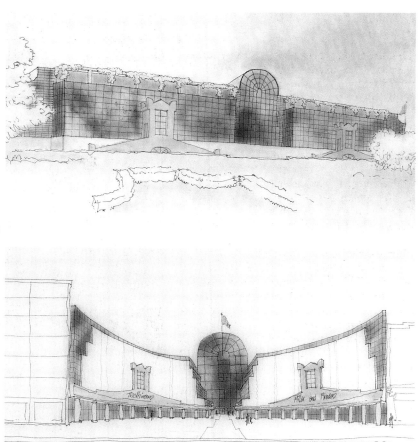

4

5

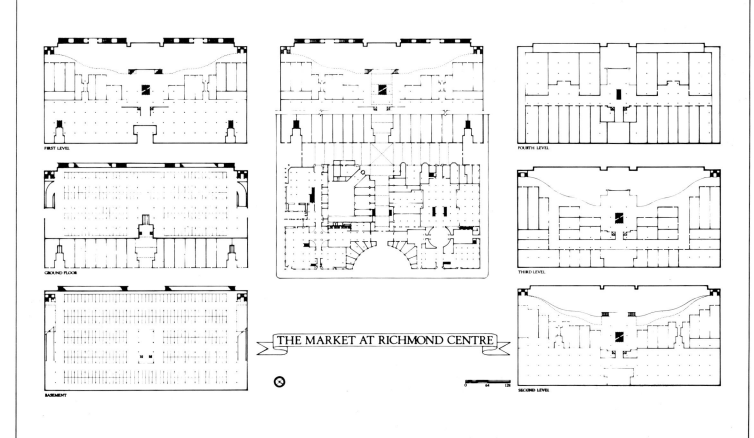

FIRST LEVEL

GROUND FLOOR

BASEMENT

FOURTH LEVEL

THIRD LEVEL

SECOND LEVEL

THE MARKET AT RICHMOND CENTRE

0   64   128

6

Houses for Corbel Properties · N.Y.

These two houses, now under construction, represent a departure from our usual practice in that, though they are purpose designed, they are not tailored to the requirements of a particular client but are conceived for sale in an affluent resort community. The wooded sites are both part of a former farm that has been sensitively subdivided. Though not visible from each other, both sites sit along the same road.

Our intention was to make two houses that used the elements of the local summer house vernacular—which is a somewhat anglicized version of the Shingle Style—to establish a sympathetic dialogue between the present and the past.

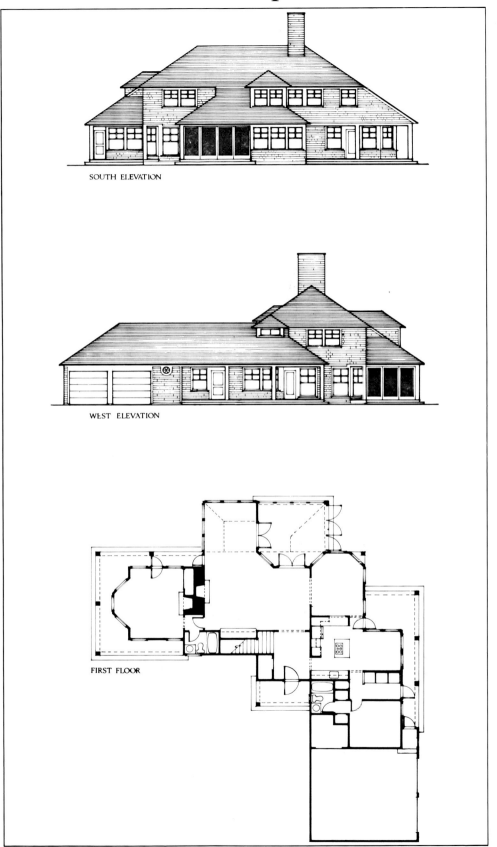

SOUTH ELEVATION

WEST ELEVATION

FIRST FLOOR

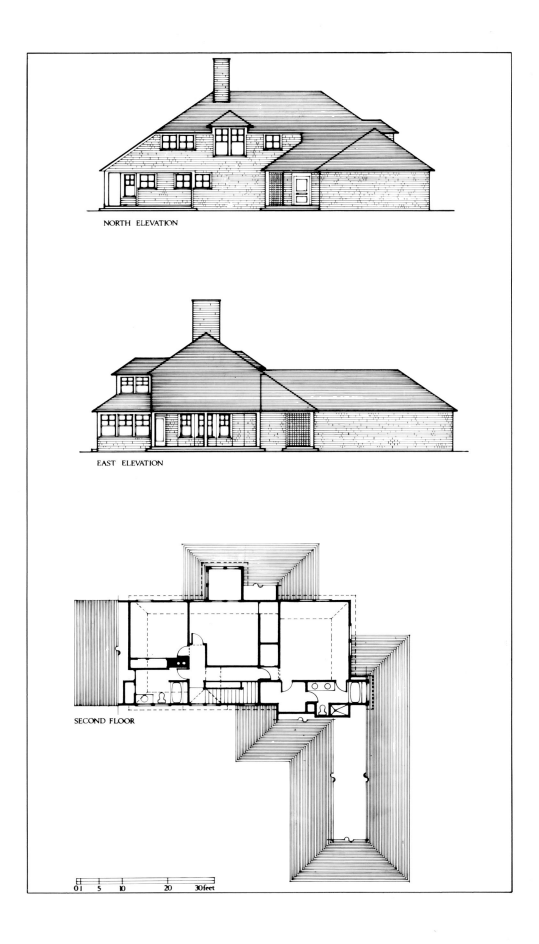

NORTH ELEVATION

EAST ELEVATION

SECOND FLOOR

0 1   5   10   20   30 feet

SOUTHWEST ELEVATION

NORTHEAST ELEVATION

NORTHWEST ELEVATION

SOUTHEAST ELEVATION

FIRST FLOOR

SECOND FLOOR

0 1 5 10 20 30 feet

N

232

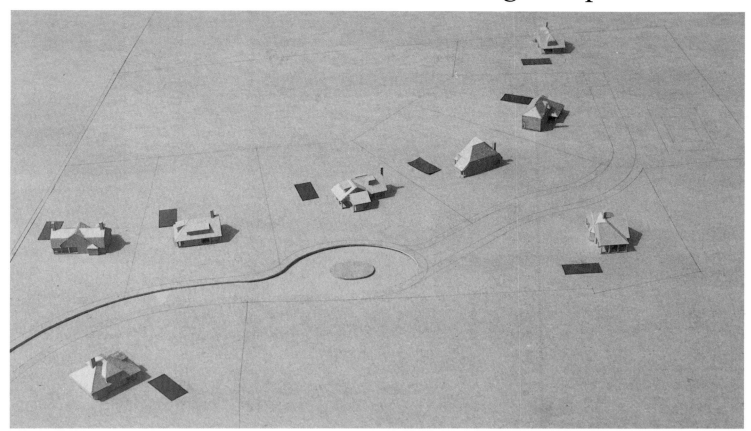

Library · San Juan Capistrano · California

Our goal in designing the public library at San Juan Capistrano is a building that responds gently to its context yet provides operational efficiency. Such a combination can go a long way towards nurturing the activities that a library shelters and the quality of life in the town as a whole. While the library responds directly to its program and immediate physical situation, it also reflects the larger stylistic current from which these surroundings are derived; in so doing, it "speaks" the traditional language of the place without using all the same words.

In organizing the library we have employed an L-shaped plan that separates and links the three principal programmatic zones of public reading, assembly, and service. The information area terminates this gallery at the east and provides a formal observational focus for the main reading and lounging areas. Organized on a symmetrical open plan basis to promote planning flexibility, the reading areas are in turn flanked by separate spaces for study, book storage, and quiet refuge. The separate wing for the quiet reading rooms forms a fountain courtyard open to the public and a walled reading patio accessible only from the library.

1. View of fountain court
2. Site plan
3. Model looking west
4. Model of the fountain court
5. Model looking south

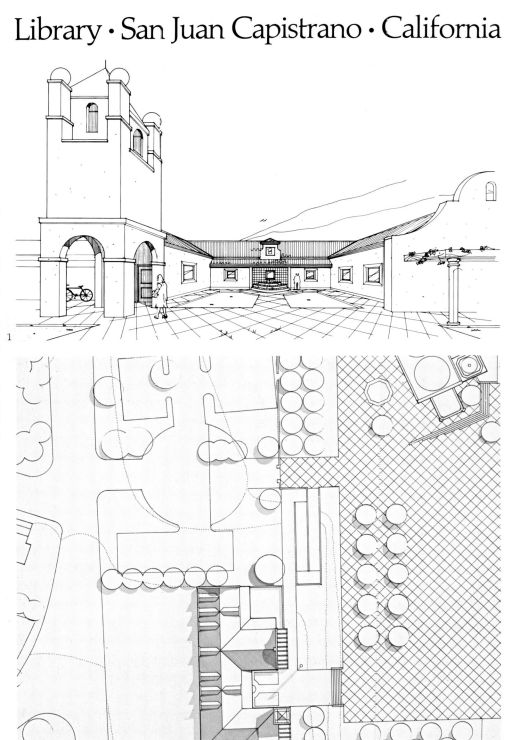

3

4

5

6

7

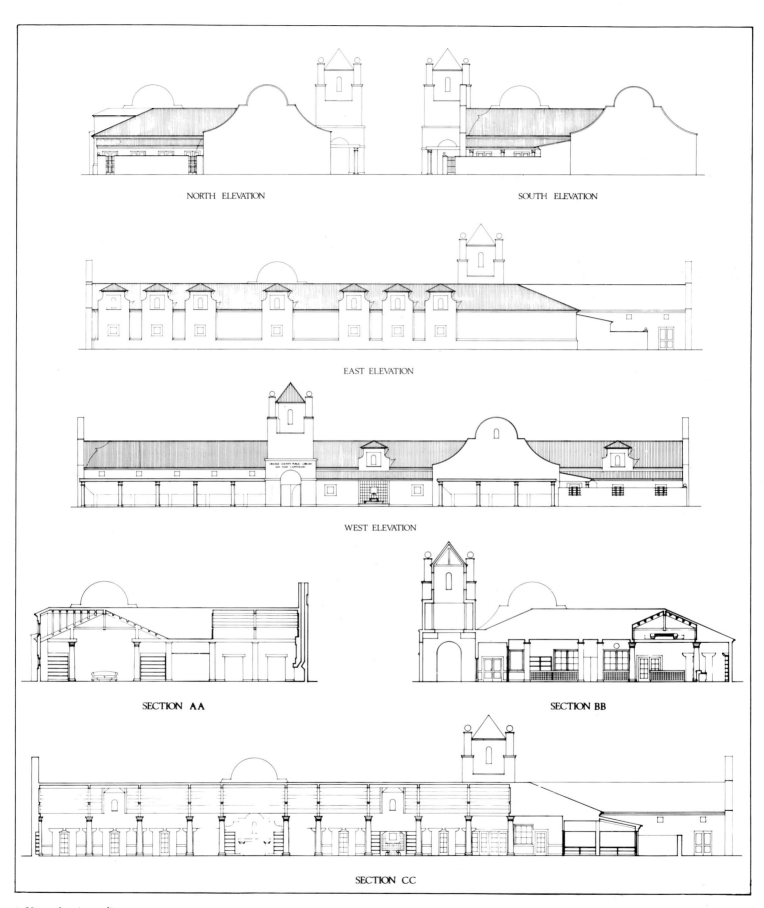

NORTH ELEVATION

SOUTH ELEVATION

EAST ELEVATION

WEST ELEVATION

SECTION AA

SECTION BB

SECTION CC

6. View of main reading room
7. View of browsing room

9

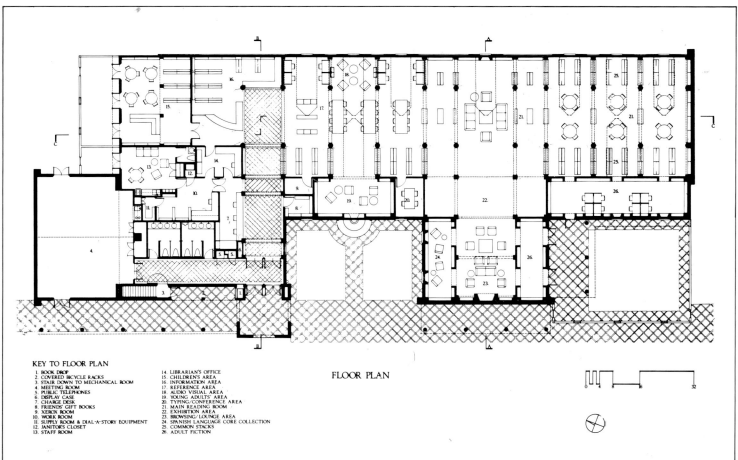

KEY TO FLOOR PLAN

1. BOOK DROP
2. COVERED BICYCLE RACKS
3. STAIR DOWN TO MECHANICAL ROOM
4. MEETING ROOM
5. PUBLIC TELEPHONES
6. DISPLAY CASE
7. CHARGE DESK
8. FRIENDS' GIFT BOOKS
9. XEROX ROOM
10. WORK ROOM
11. SUPPLY ROOM & DIAL-A-STORY EQUIPMENT
12. JANITOR'S CLOSET
13. STAFF ROOM

14. LIBRARIAN'S OFFICE
15. CHILDREN'S AREA
16. INFORMATION AREA
17. REFERENCE AREA
18. AUDIO VISUAL AREA
19. YOUNG ADULTS' AREA
20. TYPING/CONFERENCE AREA
21. MAIN READING ROOM
22. EXHIBITION AREA
23. BROWSING/LOUNGE AREA
24. SPANISH LANGUAGE CORE COLLECTION
25. COMMON STACKS
26. ADULT FICTION

FLOOR PLAN

0 4 8 16 32

11

9. Model looking southeast
10. Floor Plan
11. View from El Camino Real
12. View from information area
13. Perspective

12

13

1967-1968
Stern Apartment I, New York, New York
1967-1968
Stern Apartment II, New York, New York
1968
Gimbel Apartment, New York, New York
1969
Showroom and Offices for Tiffeau-Busch,
New York, New York
1969
Seiniger House, West Hampton, New York

1969-1970
Showrooms for Helen Harper, Inc.,
New York, New York
1969-1970
Office Addition, Long Island, New York
1970
Jenkins House, East Hampton, New York
1969-1971
White/Hoffman Apartment, New York,
New York
1970
Kozmopolitan Gallery, New York, New York

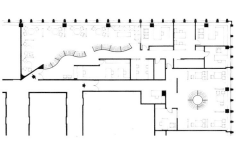 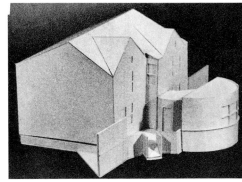

1970-1971
Traveling Exhibition, *Another Chance for Cities*
1971
Roberts Apartment, New York, New York
1971
Geary Brownstone, New York, New York
1971-1972
Kretchmer Apartment, New York, New York
1971
Residence, Gladwynne, Pennsylvania

1973
Residence, Greenwich, Connecticut
1973
Howard Apartment, New York, New York
1973
House Beautiful Living Center
1973
Marks/Friedman Apartment, New York,
New York
1973
Offices for Source Securities Corporation,
New York, New York

1973
The Architects Offices, New York, New York
1973
Godsick Apartment, New York, New York
1974
Middleton Apartment, New York, New York
1974
Model Apartment, Olympic Tower,
New York, New York
1974
House Addition, Purchase, New York

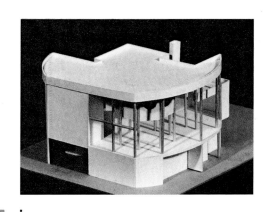

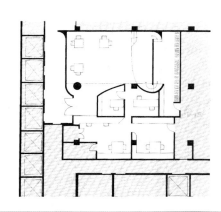

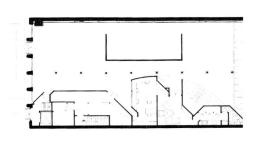

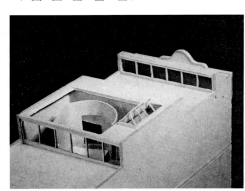

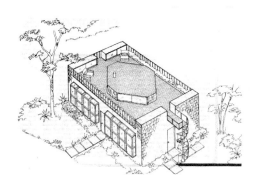

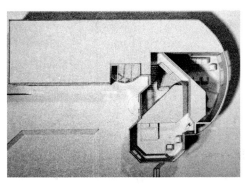

1974
Library, Museum, and Civic Plaza, Biloxi, Mississippi
1975
Regina Rail Center, Saskatchewan, Canada
1975
Collector's Apartment, New York, New York
1976
Killington Ski Lodge, Killington, Vermont
1976
Minnesota State House Extension, Minneapolis

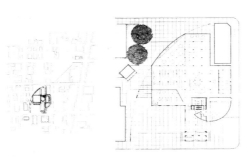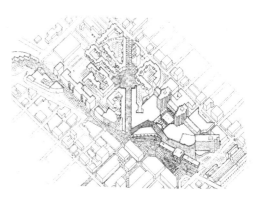

1976
Singer House Renovation, Stamford, Connecticut
1976
Student Lounge, Uris Hall, Columbia University
1977-1978
Residence, Fairfield County, Connecticut
1977
Fifth Avenue Apartment, New York, New York
1977
Reinhold Child's Room, New York, New York

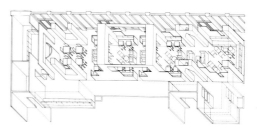

1980
Medical Loft, New York, New York
1980
Broadway Loft, New York, New York
1980
Saper House Addition, Woodstock, New York
1979-1980
Medical Offices, New York, New York
1979-1980
Contractor's Offices, Long Island City, New York

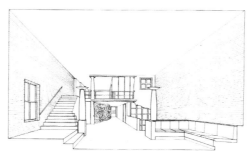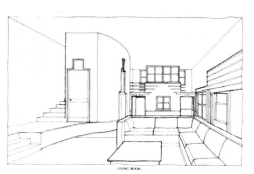

1980
East End Avenue Apartment, New York, New York
1980
Tower House, East Hampton, New York
1981
House Renovation, Kingspoint, New York
1980
Offices, Catlin and Cox, New York, New York
1980
Madison Avenue Apartment, New York City

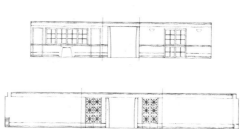

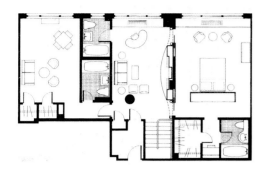

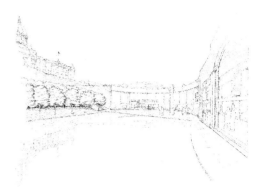

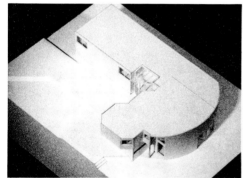

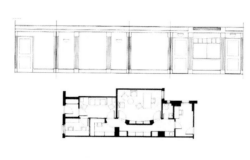

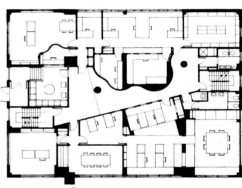

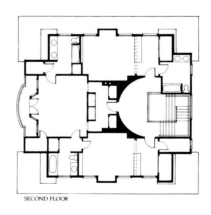

SECOND FLOOR

An Interview With Robert A.M. Stern
Dan Schneider

The following conversation took place in the offices of Robert A.M. Stern, architect, on March 17, 1981.

DBS: You were once asked if you considered yourself controversial. You replied, "I better be." For about fifteen years you have played the role of the polemicist/gadfly, the man asking questions, the man poking his finger in the belly of Modern architecture. My perspective on such matters is limited, but it seems to me you have gotten not merely results, but a great deal of acceptance. Do you still consider yourself controversial?

RAMS: Well, that ascribes to me more profundity than I am probably entitled to. The issues I've addressed and the questions I've asked are not fully answered, certainly. I think architecture has changed in the last ten years, and whether or not I've had a little part in that is for others to decide. But I would say that many, many patrons of architecture continue to build buildings and see the world in terms that I would regard as outmoded, not merely out of fashion but really quite out of joint with the issues of cities, issues of relating buildings to ideas that we have inherited from the past. I suppose I don't have to be quite as angry as when I was twenty-five, but I'm not ready for the "established old man" role.

DBS: I guess we should discuss your current work. I've seen proposals for the DOM Headquarters building in Germany, a city hall annex in Cincinnati, a museum extension on Staten Island, things like this. Aside from the emergence of an even more expressive and elaborate vocabulary, these proposals seem to reflect a strong interest in a larger, more monumental scale of design. Most of your built works have been houses, usually in a rather pastoral setting. Are you actively pursuing work in a more urban context? Can we expect a Chicago Tribune Tower in New York?

RAMS: The Chicago Tribune Tower as a drawing, as an idea, was both meant to be a comment on the idea of the original competition and on the ideology of the tall building as it has developed in the last twenty or thirty years. But the basic idea is that a reflective glass exterior can convey meanings about a building through reference to traditional forms, and that the glass itself doesn't necessarily have to lead to a blank box, which is the basic conception of the tall building that we now have. So I'd certainly be interested in having someone call me up and say, "Lets do a tall building." The reality of it is, however, that the kind of office structure that I have here...adheres to a certain American condition where you start with the relatively small buildings, houses usually, which lead to another building, and then, perhaps, to the larger commissions. Certainly offices like Breuer's or Philip Johnson's of an earlier generation conform to that pattern. Richard Meier in my own generation, though he is somewhat older than I am, conforms to that pattern, so I've decided to just dig in and be patient. At the moment, I'm rather pleased that we have a lot of work, though it's all at one scale, but the location and the issues raised by those many houses that we're working on keeps me very busy and everybody else here busy and also keeps asking many different questions of us. We also have done some work at Columbia, which you probably know....

The reason I do those competitions—sometimes they're invited, sometimes they're not—is to let the world know that I have some ideas about other scales, and also to test those ideas for myself, here in the office.

DBS: This is an intriguing notion, the implementation of Post-Modern design concepts in technoid materials developed during the Modern movement, and in the case of reflective glass, materials that are an integral part of a contemporary schlock vocabulary. It's certainly in keeping with the progressive architectural thought, not just in addressing vernacular issues, but in the sense that few Post-Modern buildings have focused on the aesthetic possibilities, and they are many, of materials like pre-stressed concrete, or plastic or....

RAMS: You use the word progressive as though architecture gets better. It doesn't get better, it only changes. Maybe in the short run it gets better, in the sense that Post-Modernism tries to include in architectural expression, in form making, things that maybe Modernism threw out and that we miss, but architecture doesn't improve in the conventional sense.

DBS: Of course, but....

RAMS: And you focus on the uses of materials and I may be misinterpreting you, but I'll take the chance, that materials can dictate form, and materials suggest what is possible in architecture. I would say that form has to take into consideration materials, but the very idea, for example of the Tribune Tower project was that a traditional form could be re-interpreted in a material that was more related to everyday technology. Pre-stressed concrete, any other kind of concrete, any other materials are first of all relatively known, and they can by nature be made to do just about anything that the architect wants. Form has to be based on something more cultural than the materials it will be realized in.

DBS: In mentioning materials I am not attempting to resurrect the "shibboleths of functional and structural determinism."

RAMS: That was a good phrase.

DBS: It was yours. New Directions in American Architecture.

RAMS: I know. I was enjoying having it thrown back at me.

DBS: You have also said, "Architecture is a story telling or communicative art." The question becomes, "What kind of story are you telling us?" Where do you locate your subject matter?

RAMS: The subject matter of architecture is at the very heart of the quarrel between Modernism and Post-Modernism, that is, the need to go beyond Modernism to a richer expression of subject matter. Modernism is concerned with conveying the story of the building's production, how it's put together, the techniques, the materials; and the story of what happens inside the building, the function. Both of those are very important stories in architecture. We are always fascinated by how buildings are made, by why they're made, but there is another dimension to architecture, perhaps the dimension of myth....

DBS: Ah....

RAMS: Just as any story, no matter what period, usually can be re-interpreted in terms of archaic myths, and myths are reinterpreted in terms of everyday experience at any given moment, so too in architecture we re-represent certain arachaic myths of shelter, the relationship of buildings to the land, of buildings to each other; certain very basic typological models are a part of that. Also buildings have the capacity to contain or display decoration, in the form of sculpture or painting, which can communicate in a more literal way...architecture is in many ways a very inarticulate art, certainly by comparison to sculpture or painting, which can reproduce figural and natural conditions in a direct way.

So I think buildings should tell a little bit about what the architect and the client thought about putting this object in the landscape, and its relationship to other buildings around it. What they valued, what they didn't value, is recorded in the design of the new building.

DBS: Can architecture, then, choose to ignore its cultural or physical environment, to establish ideas in a vacuum?

RAMS: That's really not so much a part of the Modernism/Post-Modernism argument as it is a question of the basic nature of an architectural idea, because Modernism tends to deny that a building had a story-telling role, a role in the making of symbols; that the building was what it was. The building, by nature, has an obligation to explain and express and convey meanings besides its own inherent qualities. This already changes the nature of the Modernist argument, and this creates another set of arguments about what the building should say, what is the appropriate story for any building in any place.

DBS: I recall a lecture given by Peter Eisenman at Columbia last fall. In describing his entry for a design competition in Venice, he constructed an elaborate mythology involving extremely specific moments in the cultural and physical history of the site. You know, the garish orange of this box symbolizes some obscure 14th century alchemist, and that huge crack in the courtyard alludes to some forgotten natural catastrophe. Finally the audience, which had become confused and rabid, demanded a more cogent explanation. Eisenman then sat down, admitted he made the whole thing up on the spot, and started to talk about the notion of fiction in architecture. Perhaps

245

both you and Eisenman are concerned with "telling a story" but through different means and with drastically different results.

RAMS: I think the difference is in the representational realm, because Eisenman could construct that mythology as you describe it, and maybe it's true, but since the buildings don't seem to convey in any overtly recognizable way any of that mythology, whether he denies it or says it's all a prop or whatever, the buildings don't change, they still remain there. He is trying to point out that architecture is its own autonomous discipline. Well, I believe it is in the sense that it has its own rules of composition and its own characteristics in terms of scale and space, but it also has other conditions, and one of those is that it can convey meaning through representation; representation sometimes based on previous architecture, sometimes other things. Le Corbusier believed in the autonomous qualities of architecture in the form of the classical grid and then, in the forms he chose, in the articulation of surfaces, in certain shapes inserted in the grid, suggested ideas about the "machine."

DBS: But Corbusier was neither anti-historic nor anti-symbolic.

Rams: Perhaps he was anti-historic in his use of representation. He was trying to develop architecture that would rival the work of the past without emulating it. Very difficult in my opinion. Ultimately, I think he failed. The buildings of his that have enduring value as emotional objects as opposed to intellectual constructs are such buildings as Ronchamp, which comes very close to a representational dimension.

DBS: What about an Aldo Rossi, who concentrates on external expression and literal symbol, but within a conceptual framework diametrically opposed to yours? The Neo-Rationalists in Italy explore the ideology and meaning of the city as a collective entity, focusing on the typological form and the monument as mythical or historical anchors. The Americans, meanwhile, address the individual consumer, through style based on historical allusion and contextualism. Both groups study the semantic and symbolic implications of form, but approach the issue from opposite directions, resulting in two kinds of representation that seem to me wholly dissimilar.

RAMS: I certainly don't pretend to be a student of Italian Neo-Rationalism so-called, but I think an architect like Rossi uses archetypal forms and modulates them in rather specific ways in reference to other buildings, in places such as his Teatro del Mondo or his gateways at the [Venice] Biennale. His politics aside and the particular conditions of the two countries aside, I think that he is operating in a distinctive Post-Modernist framework, and is very much concerned that architecture convey meaning beyond its own use and its own manufacture. I think that the epigones of Rossi, as epigones often do, want to systematize him, to make him into a codifiable quantity so that they can copy him.

DBS: Rossi certainly has his sources as well, perhaps Boulée or Ledoux among others whom he interprets and to some extent translates into modern terms. At the same time his forms reflect an emphatic socio-cultural orientation, that of a communist visionary. Yet, one sees Rossi on drafting boards all over America....

RAMS: No, people's impression of Rossi, based on buildings that were built ten years ago, and not on his ideas. One would only need to meet him, and speak with him, to realize that his love of architecture, and his sense of architecture as a task of making forms and an artistic process, is very, very far from the epigone mode, which is a very hard-line, rationalist method divorced from any context. Certainly the buildings in Venice show him as a playful, responsive architect who understands space, texture...many things that can relate to a particular place and a particular time. Mind you, Rossi can be very didactic. But so can we all.

DBS: Yes. Steven Peterson argues that both the Post-Modernists and the Neo-Rationalists, while recognizing the plan as a generator of order and the facade as a generator of signs, do not attempt to identify or re-define space in a manner that goes beyond the Modernist box.

RAMS: Well, I don't agree with Steven Peterson....

DBS: You use negative space, or "poche," rather freely.

RAMS: It's a technique, one that really wasn't available to us fifteen years ago.

But first of all I would say that the reason that the Post-Modernist/Modernist debate or discussion focuses on the outside is that architecture does have a certain public responsiblity. Most people experience most buildings without ever going into them. They sit on streets, and should convey some meaning independent of their internal workings. That's a built-in problem with Modernism, which saw the facade simply as the vertical expression of the plan and the section, and nothing else beyond. For me, its never been a question—the positive quality of space has always been primary. I studied architecture under Paul Rudolph. Rudolph is a master of spatial manipulation. We studied our buildings in cross-section, before we drew plans. I could make these dazzling complicated sections....

DBS: This is something you emphasize in your studios at Columbia. "Thinking in three dimensions."

RAMS The impetus when I went to school was to study the building in section first, in plan second, and the elevation probably never. Now that's just as arbitrary as concentrating on any one of three constitutent elements, but the point I'm trying to make is that the building has to exist spatially. The revolution of the twenties in terms of space, that is, the opposition of the freely moving partitions to the grid, is certainly one of the great liberating devices in the history of architecture...more often than not used incorrectly, if one can say that. The discipline of the grid and the free wall are lost in the dialogue. The thing about Le Corbusier that one can also say is that while his plans are intricate, the spaces are actually boring. They are usually one story or two stories, with very fixed sources of light, at least in the canonical buildings. The buildings by Le Corbusier that interest me more are ones like Ronchamp, where the space is dazzlingly complex and mysterious and exciting. The Villa Savoye for me is fascinating in many ways, but spatially a complete bore.

DBS: Contextualism has been an integral component in Post-Modernist doctrine. I refer to an architecture that can acknowledge, react to and interact with its surroundings in an intriguing or appropriate manner. Can this attitude extend to the definition or creation of a new context, one without historical precedent or easily perceived character? Suburbia? Exurbia? Let's take your design for the Best Products showroom [Stern was one of six architects invited to submit a design for this Museum of Modern Art exhibition] as an example.

RAMS: Hmmm....

DBS: That's what everyone says when they see it.

RAMS: Wouldn't they like to see it built, though? Look, new contexts are exactly the place that the issue becomes most critical, that is, the issue of historical memory. When you are in a new place, in order to establish some meaning, it's human nature to try to think of other places like it, or places that are not like it but that you are familiar with and that you loved.... Depending on what part of the country you're in, the Spanish, the English....each brought their architecture and adapted it to a new place. This is a way of beginning. You start from what you know.

DBS: It's ironic that in searching for an historical or vernacular counterpart to the suburban shopping mall you chose the classical temple.

RAMS: Well, it's a complex issue, of course. The Best Products thing raises a hundred different questions. For instance, the notion of consumerism, which you touched on before. Consumerism, whether we like it or not, is challenged by the Best Products concept in a funny way. John Hightower, former director of the Museum of Modern Art, is right in stating that shopping is our most important cultural activity in America. What then are we to make of the Best Products concept, where we sit at home, open up the catalogue, decide what we want, drive to the showroom, ask for television number 7043, take it home and consume it? It eliminates all the pretense of selection, of just coming upon something in the aisle—the aisle here being the street. The building itself has to function in the context of other commercial establishments which perhaps more clearly define the condition of shopping. So the building responds to these two ideas of consumerism and tries to elevate consumerism by reference to a traditional building type, a temple. I don't know, it could have been a cathedral, or any number of traditional building types...

DBS: It certainly serves to define the act of shopping as a highly charged cultural activity, if you'll ignore the pun.

RAMS: ...Absolutely, and we tend to worship goods....

DBS: ...And so the stylized columns, and the voids between, form the legs of the "fat ladies" holding up cut-outs of wedding rings and television sets.

RAMS: ....And those elements are organized left to right as you stand facing the building to describe a cycle of life, so that the icongraphic implications of the building are addressed. It's not very complicated. Through memory, through shape, through iconography, it's a building that can be read on many different levels, so it's a rich

247

building. It's certainly richer in content than the kind of things Best is building now, where brick walls crumble, or corners slide out...architectural one-liners at best, not to make a pun....

DBS: Obviously you don't go for the belly laugh....

RAMS: ...I don't usually try to. I try to be a little more ironic and a little more insidious.... Civilization has to have an ironic dimension. Otherwise, well....

DBS: The irony is unavoidable.

RAMS: I think that's one of the meanings of being modern in the broad, general sense, in the sense I have tried to define Modern architecture. I mean we view everything we do ironically because we view everything against the foibles and triumphs of people in the past. We're always pitting ourselves against them, imagining ourselves as figures in history.

DBS: In other words, in famous other words, modern life is "complex and contradictory." What if there had been no Robert Venturi?

RAMS: Well, I think Venturi made it possible for many of us to see things in a new way. His book *Complexity and Contradiction in Architecture,* and his buildings, crystallized these issues in many ways that were unimaginable before. I was particularly fortunate to know him when I was a student...I read the manuscript of *Complexity and Contradiction* before it was published and included portions in *Perspecta.* "Present at the creation" is, I suppose, the correct phrase. I've learned a lot, most importantly not to copy Bob Venturi, but to try to do what he did and does, which is to go to earlier, more archaic conditions of architecture, to read the situation of a contemporary problem in terms of a traditional set of values but not to imagine that it can just be brought forward whole, and redone as a kind of dialogue across time. Certainly that's my interpretation, or the part of Venturi's argument that is most useful for me. It certainly is a complicated argument, one that in his own work results in a kind of double direction. Some of his buildings are rather strident and billboard-like, others are rather beautifully wrought objects. The difference in those buildings does not always relate, in my opinion, to contextual issues. I don't always understand how he makes one judgment versus the other.

I suppose I've been lucky because I've not only been "present at the creation," but I am of sufficiently lively and aggressive and inquiring temperment to maybe make a few things happen on my own. I'm just not given to sitting around and observing. I jump in, which is of course something I encourage my students to do.

DBS: In your writing you draw parallels between contemporary architects and what you consider their literary counterparts. You have mentioned John Gardner, others have mentioned Bernard Malamud, or William Styron as in many ways expressing attitudes towards the creative process that are similar to yours, a "traditional Post-Modernism." Could you elaborate on this point? What are you reading these days?

RAMS: Yes, I went through my John Gardner phase. Mostly I read detective novels these days...the truth of the matter, if you want to know what I'm reading now, is Henry James. But what direct connection one could make between my architecture and the writings of Henry James is beyond me.

DMS: Some say he destroyed the "novel of ideas."

RAMS: Maybe I'm ignoring the architecture of ideas of favor of the architecture of architecture—the architecture of spatial excitement. Eisenman is more involved with the architecture of ideas. You need a thirty minute lecture for a three minute experience.

Ultimately, architecture has to stand on its own two feet, despite ideas which might be brought upon it. But I guess I like James because James burrows into the psychology of an occasion. I try, as part of the story-telling aspect of architecture, to imagine a psychology of the occasion in reference to the building. Not the psychology of an individual, but more what society expects a building to be like. If I describe for you a building, and where it's going to be built, in your mind you imagine a certain kind of building. Everybody does. For a long time architects tried to produce designs that definitely bore no similarity to what someone would imagine was appropriate, as though to fly in the face of expectation was to be somehow superior. But you'll be happy to know I've gotten over reading *The Great Gatsby* every year.

DBS: Oh my God....

RAMS: I don't do that anymore.

DBS: One more question. Many have felt the sting of your biting architectural wit. But what about that belly-laugh? Tell me a good architectural joke.

RAMS: [laughing] No. No. I don't know any architectural jokes. Jokes are one-liners really. They don't stay with you. But the wit of the eighteenth century continues to stimulate us....[end of tape].

Bibliography

Significant Publications of Office Work

Charles Moore, "Lang Residence: Where are We Now, Vincent Scully?", *Progressive Architecture* (April 1975), cover, pp. 78-83;

Paul Goldberger, "Allusions of Grandeur", *New York Times Magazine* (June 8, 1975), pp. 66-67, 72;

Suzanne Stephens, "Roosevelt Island Housing Competition: This Side of Habitat", *Progressive Architecture* (July 1975), pp. 58-59, 61;

"Stern & Hagmann: Una Residenza a Washington, Conn., 1974", *Controspazio*, Milan (September 1975), pp. 48-57;

"The Work of Robert A.M. Stern and John S. Hagmann", Special Feature, *Architecture and Urbanism*, (Tokyo, October 1975), cover, pp. 85-150;

Deborah Nevins, editor, "The Roosevelt Island Housing Competition", Architectural League of New York, 1975;

Diana Agrest and Alessandra Latour, "Sviluppo Urbano e Forma Della Citta a New York" (Roosevelt Island Competition), *Controspazio*, Milan (December 1975), cover, pp. 8-15;

Sharon Lee Ryder , "Stern Dimensions", *Progressive Architecture* (June 1976), pp. 70-77;

Barbara Radice & Franco Raggi, editors, Catalog "La Biennale di Venezia", Section on Visual Arts and Architecture, Venice: Alfieri Edizioni d'Arte, 1976, Volume II, pp. 262-266;

Douglas Davis with Mary Rourke, "Real Dream Houses", *Newsweek* (October 4, 1976), pp. 68-69;

Luis Domenich, "Stern Star Estrella: La Obra de Robert A.M. Stern", *Arquitecturas Bis*, Barcelona (September 1976), pp. 12-25;

"Meet the Architect, Robert A.M. Stern", *Global Architecture Houses #1*, Tokyo, cover, pp. 36-77;

Suzanne Stephens, "Grand Allusions", *Progressive Architecture* (February 1977), pp. 58-63;

Jane Holtz Kay, "The Stern View", *Building Design* (February 11, 1979), pp. 16-17;

Charles Jencks, "More Modern Than Modern", *The Sunday Times Magazine* (May 29, 1977), pp. 30-31;

Charles Jencks, *The Language of Post-Modern Architecture* London, 1977;

Paul Goldberger, "Robert A.M. Stern's Two Houses", *Architecture and Urbanism*, (September 1977), pp. 81-92;

"Stern Hybrids", *The Architectural Review* (December 1977), pp. 331-333;

Martin Filler, "Making It Legal", *Progressive Architecture* (March 1978), pp. 64-65;

Douglas Davis, "Design for Living", *Newsweek* (November 6, 1978), pp. 82-91;

"Les Grandes Demeures" *L'Architecture D'Aujourd'hui* (December 1978), pp. 61-64;

Robert Hughes, "U.S. Architects: Doing Their Own Things", *Time Magazine*, (January 8, 1979), pp. 52-59;

Barry Dean, "Architectural Ornamentation", *Residential Interiors* (September/October 1979), pp. 88-92;

Douglas Davis, "Playful Facades", *Newsweek* (January 28, 1980). pp. 75-76;

Eleni Constantine, "Ace of Clubs", *Progressive Architecture* (September 1979), pp. 61-64;

Building for BEST Products (Catalog), The Museum of Modern Art, New York, N.Y. 1979; pp. 26-29

Brent Brolin, *Architecture in Context*, Van Nostrand Reinhold Co., New York, N.Y. 1980, pp. 15, 25, 75, 128-129, 138, 140;

"Residence and Outbuildings", *Precis* Vol. 2, 1980, pp. 56-57;

Gabriella Bordano, (ed.), *The Presence of the Past*, La Biennale de Venezia, Milani, Electa Editrice, 1980, pp. 9, 15, 16, 29, 31, 34, 38, 61, 289-294, 306;

Charles Jencks, *Post Modern Classicism*, Academy Editions, London, England, 1980, pp. 11, 35-42;

Barbaralee Diamonstein, (ed.) *Artists and Architects Collaboration*, Whitney Library of Design, New York, 1981, pp. 115-116;

Helmuth Gsollpointner, Angela Hareiter, Laurids Ortner (editors), *Design Ist Unsichbar*, Osterreichisches Institut fur visuelle Gestaltung, Locker Verlag, Linz, Austria (Catalog for Forum Design Exhibition) 1981, pp. 259-273;

Helen Searing, Henry Hope Read (editors), *A New Classicism: American Architecture Now*, Smith College Museum of Art, Northampton, Mass. 1981, pp. 50-52;

"Five Projects of Robert A.M. Stern", *A+U* No. 129, June 1981, pp. 13-22;

Vincent Scully, "The Star in Stern: Sightings and Orientation", in David Dunster (ed.) *Robert Stern*, Academy Editions, London, England, 1981.

250

Publications in Periodicals

"PSFS: Beaux Arts Theory and Rational Expressionism", *Journal of the Society of Architectural Historians*, (May 1962), pp. 84-102;

"Relevance of the Decade 1929-1939", *Journal of the Society of Architectural Historians* (March 1965);

"Paul Rudolph: the First Twenty-Five Years", *Kokusai Kenchiku* International Architecture, Tokyo (May 1965);

Editor, *Perspecta, the Yale Architectural Journal 9/10* (1965);

"Office of Earl P. Carlin", *Perspecta* (1965);

"Constitution Plaza One Year After", *Progressive Architecture* (December 1965), pp. 166-171;

"A Static Gallery", book review, *Progressive Architecture* (April 1966), p. 234;

"Random Shots at USA '65", book review, *Progressive Architecture* (May 1966), pp. 264, 266;

"Stompin' at the Savoye", criticism, *Architectural Forum* (May 1973), pp. 46-48;

"Tape Recorder Chats", book review, *Architectural Record* (May 1973), pp. 43-45;

"Raymond Hood", book review, *Progressive Architecture* (July 1974), pp. 110-114;

"Yale 1950-1965", *Oppositions 4* (October 1974), pp. 35-62;

"Toward an Architecture of Symbolic Assemblage", *Progressive Architecture* (April 1975), pp. 72-77;

Guest Editor, *Architecture and Urbanism* (Tokyo, April 1975), Special Feature "White and Gray", pp. 25-180;

"A Serious Discussion of an Almost Whimsical House", *Architectural Record* (July 1975), pp. 99-104;

"Park Avenue is Almost All Right (Maybe)", book review, *Architectural Record* (February 1976), p. 43;

"Letter to the Editor", *Oppositions 7* (Winter 1976), p. 17;

"Robert Stern on Jim Stirling", interview, *Design Quarterly 100* (Spring 1976), p. 26;

"Gray Architecture; Quelques Variations Post-Modernistes Autour de l'Orthodoxie", *l'Architecture d'Aujourd-hui* (Paris, August/September 1976), p. 83;

"Stern Star Estrella: la Obrade Robert A.M. Stern", *Arquitecturas Bis*, vol. 15, Luis Domenech (September 1976), pp. 12-25;

Guest Editor, *Architecture and Urbanism* (Tokyo, January 1977) Special Feature "40 Under 40 + 10";

"At the Edges of Modernism", *Architectural Design*, vol. 47, no. 4 (April 1977), pp. 274-286;

"Forum: The Beaux-Arts Exhibition", *Oppositions 8* (Spring 1977), pp. 169-171;

"Letter to the Editor", *Contract Interiors* (July 1977), p. 6;

"Further Thoughts on Millbank", *Architectural Design* (with George Baird and Charles Jencks), no. 47 (July/August 1977), pp. 543-4;

"Venturi and Rauch: Learning to Love Them", *Architectural Monographs*, Vol. 1 (1978), pp. 93-94;

"New Directions in Modern American Architecture, Postscript", *Architectural Association Quarterly*, Vol. 9, nos. 2 & 3, (1978), pp. 66-71;

"The Suburban Alternative: Coping with the Middle City", *Architectural Record* (August 1978), pp. 93-100;

"How to Redesign New York", *Art News*, vol. 78, No. 9 (November 1978), pp. 81-82;

"Models for Reality: Some Observations", *Great Models*, the student publications of the School of Design, North Carolina State University, No. 27 (1978), pp. 72-75;

"Drawing from Models", (with Frances Halsband, R.M. Kliment, and Richard B. Oliver), *Journal of Architectural Education*, vol. XXXII, No. 1 (September 1978), p. 7;

"Not Spaces but...Rooms", *Global House #5* (December 1978), pp. 4-7;

"Modern Housing Dwelling Units", book review, *Architectural Record* (June 1979), p. 208;

"Doubles of Post-Modern", *Harvard Architectural Review*, vol. 1 (Spring 1980), pp. 74-87

"After the Modern Movement", *Parametro*, No. 72, pp. 36-40;

Comments, "The 27th P/A Awards", Jury member, *Progressive Architecture*, January 1980, pp. 90-125;

"With Rhetoric: The New York Apartment House", *VIA*, vol. IV (1980), pp. 78-111;

Charles Gandee , ed., "Behind the Facades: A Conversation with Robert A.M. Stern", *Architectural Record*, (March 1981), pp. 108-113;

"Post Profligate Architecture—Some Observations in the Waning of the Petroleum Era", *American Architecture After Modernism A + U, Special Issue*, (March 1981), pp. 8-15;

Daralice Donkervoet , ed., "An Interview with Robert A.M. Stern", *CRIT The Architectural Student Journal*, (Spring 1981), pp. 19-21;

Daniel Schneider , ed., "Robert Stern Interview" *UPSTART* Columbia University, New York, N.Y. 1981;

Jay Murphy , ed., "Interview Robert A.M. Stern", *Dimensions*, Volume II, No. 1, College of Architecture, University of Nebraska at Lincoln, 1981, pp. 6-10.

Books by Robert A. M. Stern

40 Under 40: Young Talent in Architecture (exhibition catalog), New York, American Federation of Arts, 1966;

New Directions in American Architecture, New York, Braziller, 1969; expanded 2nd edition 1977 (also published in Italian, Spanish and Japanese);

George Howe: Toward a Modern American Architecture, New Haven, Yale University Press, 1975;

Guest Editor, Special Feature "White and Grey", *Architecture and Urbanism*, Japan, 1975;

Introduction, *The PSFS Building* (PSFS Booklet), Philadelphia, May, 1976;

Forward (with Wilder Green), David Gebhard and Deborah Nevins, *200 Years of American Architectural Drawings*, New York, Whitney Library of Design, 1977;

Guest Editor, Special Feature "40 Under 40+10", *Architecture and Urbanism*, Japan, January, 1977;

Commentary, *Philip Johnson: Collected Writings*, New York, Oxford University Press, 1979;

"A Conversation with Robert Stern; March 29, 1979, in David Park Curry and Patricia Dawes Pierce, *Monument: The Connecticut State Capitol*, Old State House Association, Hartford, 1979, pp. 89-97;

Co-author (with Deborah Nevins), *The Architect's Eye: American Architectural Drawings From 1799-1978*, New York, Pantheon, 1979;

Interview, in Barbaralee Diamonstein, *American Architecture Now*, Rizzoli International Publications Inc., 1980, pp. 230-253.

Credits and Acknowledgements for Selected Works

Wiseman House, Montauk, New York 1965-67

Residence, East Hampton, New York 1968-69
Assistants: Jonathan Stoumen, Craig W. Whitaker

Poolhouse, Purchase, New York 1970-71
With John S. Hagmann
Assistant: Steven Foote

Residence, Montauk, New York 1971-72
With John S. Hagmann
Assistants: John Anhorn, Daniel L.Colbert

Rooftop Apartment, New York City 1973
Assistant-in-Charge: Daniel L. Colbert
Assistant: Ronne Fisher

Duplex Apartment, New York City 1973
With John S. Hagmann
Assistants: Ronne Fisher, Ralph Frishman, Jeremy P. Lang

Residence, East Hampton, New York, 1973-75
With John S. Hagmann
Assistants: John Anhorn, Joan Chan, Daniel L. Colbert

New York Brownstone, New York, N.Y. 1972-79
Assistant-in-Charge: Wayne Berg
Assistants: Mark Mariscal Jean Wall, Robert Tolmach

Lang Residence, Washington, Connecticut 1973-74
With John S. Hagmann
Assistant-in-Charge: Jeremy P. Lang
Assistant: Edmund H. Stoecklein

Poolhouse, Greenwich, Connecticut 1973-74
With John S. Hagmann
Assistant-in-Charge: Daniel L. Colbert
Assistants: Joan Chan, Ronne Fisher, William Schweber, Clifford M. Thacher-Renshaw

Residence, North Stamford, Connecticut 1975
With John S. Hagmann
Assistant-in-Charge: Jeremy P. Lang
Assistant: Ronne Fisher

Residence, Westchester County, New York 1974-75
With John S. Hagmann
Assistant-in-Charge: Daniel L. Colbert, Jeremy P. Lang
Assistants: Robert Buford, Joan Chan, Ronne Fisher

New York Townhouse, New York City 1974-75
Assistant-in-Charge: Jeremy Lang
Assistants: Wayne Berg, Ronne Fisher, Laurence Marner

Apartment, Elkins Park, Pennsylvania 1975
With John S. Hagmann
Assistants: Joan Chan, Ronne Fisher

Roosevelt Island Competition, New York 1975
With John S. Hagmann
Assistant-in-Charge: Wayne Berg
Assistants: Robert Buford, Daniel L. Colbert, Gregory Gall, Jeremy P. Lang, Laurence Marner, Joan Oxenfelt, Edmund H. Stoecklein, Clifford M. Thacher-Renshaw

Jerome Greene Hall, Columbia University 1975
With John S. Hagmann
Assistant: Wayne Berg

Residence, Long Island, New York 1975-76
With John S. Hagmann
Assistants: Clifford M. Thacher-Renshaw, Ronne Fisher

Riviera Beach, Suburb, Florida 1976
With John S. Hagmann
Assistant-in-Charge: Wayne Berg
Assistants: Kyle Johnson, Edmund H. Stoecklein

Biennale Facade, Venice, Italy 1980
Assistant-in-Charge: Gavin Macrae-Gibson
Assistants: Mark Albert, Peter Pennoyer

Chicago Tribune Competition 1980
Assistant-in-Charge: Gavin Macrae-Gibson
Assistants: Mark Albert, Charles D. Warren

Classical Duplex Apartment, New York City 1980
Assistant-in-Charge: Gavin Macrae-Gibson
Assistants: Terry Brown, Alan Gerber

Ferris Booth Hall, Columbia University 1980
Assistant-in-Charge: Anthony Cohn
Assistant: Mark Mariscal

City Hall Annex, Cincinatti, Ohio 1980
Assistants: Gregory Bader, Charles D. Warren

Residence, Farm Neck, Massachusetts 1980
Assistant-in-Charge: Roger H. Seifter
Assistant: John Krieble
Assistant-in-Charge of interiors: Ronne Fisher

Garibaldi Meucci Museum Competition 1980
Assistant-in-Charge: Charles D. Warren
Assistant: Anthony Cohn

Collaboration, With Robert Graham 1980
Sculpture: Robert Graham
Assistant-in-Charge: Charles D. Warren

DOM Corporation Headquarters, Bruhl Germany 1980
Assistant-in-Charge: John Ike
Assistants: John Averitt, Terry Brown, Peter Pennoyer

Peaceable Kingdom Barn, Texas 1976
Assistant: Edmund H. Stoecklein

Subway Suburb 1976-80
Assistants: Mark Albert, Wayne Berg, Edmund H. Stoecklein, Charles D. Warren

Housing for the Elderly, Brookhaven, N.Y. 1976
Assistant-in-Charge: Wayne Berg
Assistants: Daniel L. Colbert, Gregory M. Gall, Duncan Hazard, Edmund H. Stoecklein, Clifford M. Thacher-Renshaw

Park Avenue Apartment, New York City 1977
Assistants: Ronne Fisher, Clifford M. Thacher-Renshaw

10th Anniversary Poster, IAUS 1977
Assistant: Mark Mariscal

Residence, Deal, New Jersey, 1977-78
Assistant-in-Charge: Daniel Colbert
Assistant: Mark Mariscal

Erbun Fabrics Showroom, New York City 1978
Assistant: Ethelind Coblin

1st Avenue Squash Club, New York City 1978
Assistant: Mark Mariscal

Residence at East Hampton 1980
Assistant-in-Charge: Terry Brown
Assistants: John Claggett, Peter Pennoyer
Assistant-in-Charge (interiors): Ronne Fisher

Young Hoffman Exhibition, Chicago 1981
Assistant-in-Charge: Anthony Cohn
Assistant: Erica Millar

Residence, Locust Valley, New York 1980-81
Assistant-in-Charge: Charles D. Warren
Assistants: Perry Kulper, Whitney Sander

Richmond Centre, Richmond, Virginia 1981
Assistant-in-Charge: Charles D. Warren
Also participating: Faculty and students of School of Architecture, Mississippi State University, Starkville MI.
Faculty Assistants: Henry Hildebrandt, Ronald W. Murray
Student Assistants: G. Allen, T. Blackwell J. Brown, S. Creevy, A. Gieger, S. Jackson, D. Landry, S. Mohon, L. McCool, A. Roberts, L. Robertson, A. Smith, W. Smith, R. Vanlandingham

Houses for Corbel Properties 1981
Assistant-in-Charge: Roger H. Seifter

Library, San Juan Capistrano, California 1980
Assistant-in-Charge: John Averitt, Roger H. Seifter
Assistants: Terry Brown, Anthony Cohn, Randy Correll, John Ike, Erica Millar, Peter Pennoyer

Photo Credits

Fresh Cafe, New York City 1978
Assistant: Mark Mariscal
Residence, East Hampton, New York 1979
Assistant-in-Charge: Roger H. Seifter
Assistant: Mark Mariscal
Redtop, Dublin, New Hampshire 1978
Assistant-in-Charge: Ethelind Coblin
Assistant: Roger H. Seifter
**Gramercy Park Apartment,
New York City** 1979
Assistant in Charge: Ethelind Coblin
Assistants: Alan Gerber, Mark Mariscal
International House, New York City 1979
Assistant-in-Charge: Roger H. Seifter
Assistants: John Krieble, Gavin Macrae-
Gibson
Super Spa, Bathing Pavillion 1979
Assistants: Gregory Bader, Terry Brown,
John Ike, Gavin Macrae-Gibson,
Charles D. Warren
**Inner Dune Residence, East Hampton,
New York** 1979-80
Assistant: Gregory Bader
Residence, Llewellyn Park, New Jersey
1979
Assistants: Ethelind Coblin, Anthony
Cohn, Alan Gerber, Gavin Macrae-
Gibson
Residence, Chilmark 1980
Assistant-in-Charge: Roger H. Seifter
Assistants: John Krieble, Alan Gerber
Best Products, Catalogue Showroom, 1979
Assistant-in-Charge: Gavin Macrae-
Gibson
Assistants: Mark Albert, John Ike,
Charles D. Warren
**Lawson Residence, East Quoque,
New York** 1979
Assistants: John Averitt, Terry Brown,
John Krieble
Temple of Love 1979
Assistant: Ethelind Coblin
Prototype Housing 1980
Assistant: Gavin Macrae-Gibson
Residence King's Point, New York 1980
Assistants: John Averitt, Terry Brown
Design Pavilion, Linz, Austria 1980
Assistant-in-Charge: Gavin Macrae-
Gibson
Assistants: Mark Albert, Peter Pennoyer
Visitor's Center, Shaker Village, Kentucky
1980
Assistants: John Averitt, Ethelind Coblin

Mark Albert 156-6, 156-7, 158-3, 159-4,
159-5, 159-6, 159-7, 176-5, 198-1
Terry Brown 201-1, 200-2, 201-6, 202-8,
203-12, 203-13
Anthony Cohn 164-6, 166-9, 166-10,
166-11, 167-12, 167-12, 167-14, 168-15,
168-16, 168-17, 168-18, 168-19, 169-21,
169-22, 169-23, 183-4
Wolfgang Hoyt/Esto 175-3
Y. Futagawa 28-5, 87-3, 88-4, 88-5, 88-6,
90-10
John T. Hill 27-2, 27-4
Bob Kiss 4-1
John Krieble 160-1, 161-3, 161-6, 162-7,
163-8
Jeremy P. Lang 74-1, 75-3, 76-5, 76-6,
77-7, 77-8
Maris/Semel 30-1, 30-2, 31-3, 31-4, 31-5,
32-6, 32-7, 34-1, 34-2, 35-3, 36-5, 36-6,
37-9, 38-11, 39-14, 39-15, 241-9, 241-14,
240-21, 243-34
Mark Mariscal 52-1, 53-4, 55-7, 55-8,
56-10, 130-1, 131-3, 131-5, 138-1, 138-2,
140-1, 142-4, 142-5, 144-11, 144-12, 144-13,
144-14, 240-2, 240-11
Norman McGrath 44-1, 45-3, 53-3, 53-5,
55-9, 83-18
Hans Namuth 18-1, 19-2, 19-3, 20-4,
23-9, 24-10, 25-11, 29-6, 240-1
Office of Robert A.M. Stern 116-1, 132-1,
132-2, 187-4, 187-5, 192-1, 192-2, 197-6,
226-2, 241-5, 240-7, 241-8, 240-12,
241-13, 241-15, 240-17, 241-20, 240-22,
242-31, 243-35, 243-38, 242-41
Peter M. Pennoyer 82-15, 157-9, 191-6,
202-7, 202-9, 203-11
Tim Street-Porter 127-3
Robert A.M. Stern 22-8, 26-1, 27-3,
50-5, 78-1, 105-6, 128-1, 129-2, 131-4,
136-1, 137-2, 137-3, 137-4, 146-1, 147-4,
147-7, 149, 167-13, 170-1, 170-2, 171-4,
172-5, 172-6, 178-1, 179-2, 179-3, 183-3,
190-1, 194-1, 196-3, 196-4
**Retoria/Y. Futagawa & Associates
Photographers—T. Kitajima** 54-6
**Retoria/Y. Futagawa & Associates
Photographers—Y. Takase** 72-1, 73-8,
73-9
Don Richards 142-3
James V. Righter 73-4
Whitney Sander 211-2, 211-3, 222-3,
226-2, 233-3, 233-4
Spinelli 182-1, 182-2

E. Stocklein 40-1, 42-3, 42-4, 42-5, 43-6,
43-7, 46-6, 46-7, 47-8, 47-9, 48-1, 48-2,
49-3, 50-6, 50-7, 58-1, 58-2, 59-3, 60-6,
61-8, 61-9, 62-10, 63-13, 63-14, 64-15,
64-16, 65-18, 66-1, 67-2, 67-3, 68-5, 70-9,
71-11, 78-2, 79-3, 79-4, 79-5, 79-6, 79-7,
81-11, 81-12, 82-13, 82-14, 82-16, 82-17,
83-20, 83-21, 85-28, 85-29, 87-3, 89-8,
89-9, 90-10, 91-11, 91-12, 91-13, 91-14,
92-15, 94-1, 94-2, 94-3, 95-4, 96-5, 97-7,
98-1, 98-2, 98-3, 102-12, 103-13, 103-14,
105-7, 105-8, 106-1, 106-2, 107-3, 107-4,
109-8, 110-10, 111-11, 111-12, 112-1, 112-2,
113-3, 122-1, 122-2, 123-4, 133-4, 134-1,
135-2, 150-1, 151-2, 151-6, 152-4, 153-6,
153-7, 154-1, 155-3, 157-10, 174-2, 175-3,
204-1, 206-4, 206-5, 207-6, 207-7, 214-1,
215-2, 216-1, 218-6, 218-7, 218-8, 219-10,
235-3, 235-4, 235-5, 238-8, 241-19, 241-29
Clifford M. Thacher-Renshaw 126-1
Donald Young 224-1

I would especially like to thank Erica Millar
and Jenny Moncayo of Robert Stern's office
for their assistance in compiling the materials. I am also indebted to Sharon Pachter
for her devotion and perseverance in the
production of this book.

P.A.